BOOST YOUR SKILLS

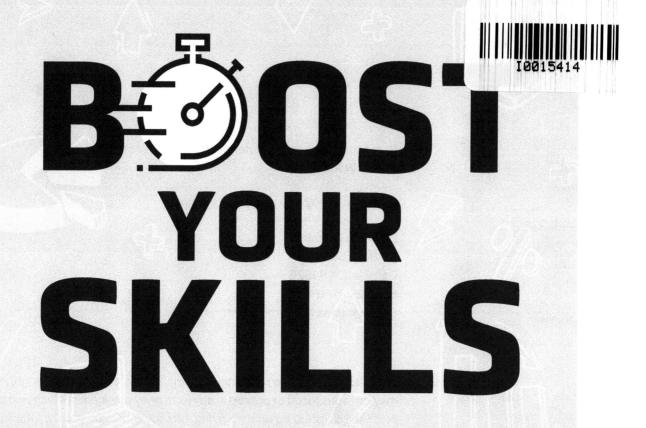

in Computer Basics for ESL Learners

Lois Wooden

LABYRINTH

LEARNING®

Co-Founder:
Brian Favro

Product Manager:
Jason Favro

Development Manager:
Laura Popelka

Production Manager:
Debra Grose

Senior Editor:
Alexandra Mummery

eLearning Specialist:
Lauren Carlson

Editorial Team:
Linda Simpson, Donna Bacidore

Interior Design:
Debra Grose

Cover Design:
Sam Anderson Design

LABYRINTH
LEARNING™

Boost Your Skills In Computer Basics for ESL Learners
By Lois Wooden

Copyright © 2024 by Labyrinth Learning

Labyrinth Learning
PO Box 2669
Danville, CA 94526
800.522.9746
On the web at: lablearning.com

ITEM: 1-64061-577-6
ISBN-13: 978-1-64061-577-9

Table of Contents

Preface . . . . *v*

CHAPTER 1
Computer Basics 1
Vocabulary. 2
    Picture Dictionary – Nouns 2
    Computer Verbs. 4
Concepts and Exercises. 5
    How We Use Computers 5
    Parts of the Computer 6
    The Correct Way to Sit at the Computer 7
    Turning On the Computer 8
    What Is Windows?. 9
    Using a Mouse 11
    Turning Off the Computer 13
Skill Builder Exercises. 14
Paired Conversation. 16
Chapter Review 17

CHAPTER 2
Windows and the Start Menu. 21
Vocabulary. 22
    Picture Dictionary – Nouns 22
    Computer Verbs. 24
Concepts and Exercises. 25
    The Windows Desktop 25
    Opening Programs 26
    Parts of a Program Window. 28
    Moving a Window. 30
Skill Builder Exercises. 32
Paired Conversation. 33
Chapter Review 34

CHAPTER 3
Windows Programs 37
Vocabulary. 38
    Picture Dictionary – Nouns 38
    Computer Verbs. 40
Concepts and Exercises. 41
    Common Features in Programs. 41
    Dialog Boxes. 44
    Using Ribbon Tools 46
    The Windows Calculator. 51
    Using Menus. 54
Skill Builder Exercises. 56
Paired Conversation 60
Chapter Review 61

CHAPTER 4
Creating a Document in Word 63
Vocabulary. 64
    Picture Dictionary – Nouns 64
    Computer Verbs. 66
Concepts and Exercises. 67
    The Computer Keyboard 67
    Using the Keyboard 69
    Word-Processing Programs 70
    Inserting Text. 72
    Deleting Text 73
    Printing Your Work. 75
Skill Builder Exercises. 77
Paired Conversation. 81
Chapter Review 82

CHAPTER 5

More with Word 85

Vocabulary. 86
    Picture Dictionary – Nouns 86
    Computer Verbs. 87
Concepts and Exercises. 88
    Highlighting Text 88
    Formatting Text. 90
    Bullets 92
    Alignment 94
    Saving Your Work 95
Skill Builder Exercises. 99
Paired Conversation. 103
Chapter Review 104

CHAPTER 6

The Internet 107

Vocabulary. 108
    Picture Dictionary – Nouns 108
    Computer Verbs. 110
Concepts and Exercises. 111
    What Is the Internet? 111
    Google Chrome 112
    The Address Bar. 113
    Search Engines 114
    Search Results 116
    Search for a Job Online 119
    Apply for a Job Online 121
Skill Builder Exercises. 122
Paired Conversation 125
Chapter Review. 126

CHAPTER 7

Email 129

Vocabulary. 130
    Picture Dictionary – Nouns 130
    Computer Verbs. 131
Concepts and Exercises. 132
    About Email 132
    Writing and Sending a Message. 133
    Contacts. 134
    Reading Your Email 135
    Replying to Messages 136
Skill Builder Exercises 137
Paired Conversation. 140
Chapter Review 141

CHAPTER 8

Files, Folders, and Windows Search 145

Vocabulary. 146
    Picture Dictionary – Nouns 146
    Computer Verbs. 147
Concepts and Exercises. 148
    The File Explorer Window 148
    Double-Clicking 150
    Viewing Files on a USB Drive. 152
    Creating Folders 156
    Opening Files and Saving to a New Location. . . . 158
    Taking a Screen Capture. 160
    Windows Search 163
Skill Builder Exercises. 166
Paired Conversation 170
Chapter Review 171

CHAPTER 9

Writing Letters in Word. 173

Vocabulary. 174
    Picture Dictionary – Nouns 174
    Computer Verbs. 176
Concepts and Exercises. 177
    The Word Window 177
    Typing a Personal Letter 180
    Checking Your Spelling and Grammar 183
    Typing a Business Letter. 185
    Opening a Saved File 188
Skill Builder Exercises 190
Paired Conversation 195
Chapter Review 196

CHAPTER 10

Editing Word Documents 199

Vocabulary. 200
    Picture Dictionary – Nouns 200
    Computer Verbs. 201
Concepts and Exercises. 202
    Typing a Résumé. 202
    Copying and Pasting Within a Program 205
    Saving a File with a New Name. 208
    Undo 209
    Moving Text in Word 210
    Right-Click to Copy and Paste 212
    Copying from One Program to Another 214
Skill Builder Exercises. 216
Paired Conversation. 222
Chapter Review 223

Chapter Review Answer Key 225

Preface

Boost Your Skills in Computer Basics for ESL Learners teaches the basics of effectively using the computer to perform essential tasks, while highlighting daily life skills and English reading comprehension and writing. We focus on fundamental concepts and language building, and reinforce learning through a systematic progression of exercises. Procedural reference steps, precise callouts on illustrations, step-by-step instruction, and minimal page distractions combine to create a learning solution that is highly effective.

New to this edition: This edition features updated screens for the latest look of Microsoft Windows 10 and Word, as well as Google Chrome and Gmail. The exercises dealing with the Word app may be completed using various desktop versions of Office or Office 365.

This book is designed to reach ESL/ELL learners with at least a Low Intermediate ESL reading proficiency (per the CASAS Skill Level Descriptors for ESL).

About the Author

Lois Wooden has taught high-school students and adults in Manteca, CA, since 1992. Her teaching experience includes basic computer concepts, Microsoft Office applications, the Internet, and web design. In addition, Lois has taught ESL since 2005 and has successfully completed numerous English-language civics teaching modules.

CHAPTER 1

Computer Basics

Computer Objectives

■ Turn the computer on and off

■ Name the major parts of the computer

■ Use the mouse

Language Objectives

■ Use vocabulary words to describe parts of the computer

■ Use computer verbs to describe actions

■ Talk with a partner about the computer

Learning Resources: **boostyourskills.lablearning.com**

 Vocabulary

Picture Dictionary – Nouns

A **noun** is the name of a person, place, or thing. The following nouns are introduced in this chapter:

1. **CPU (central processing unit)** – The brain of the computer system

2. **Power button** – The button that turns the computer on

3. **Monitor** – The part of the computer that you look at to see your work; like a television

4. **Screen** – The part of the monitor that lights up and shows what is happening on the computer

5. **Keyboard** – The part that you type on with all the letters, symbols, and functions

6. **Mouse** – The small oval piece that you can use to move from one part of the screen to another

7. **Mouse button** – The two parts at the top of the mouse used to control mouse movement and make selections

8. **Desktop** – The picture you see on your screen when you turn on your computer that has many program icons on it

9. **Icon** – A picture that represents a program or command

Recycle Bin

10. **Laptop** – A computer that is all one piece and easy to carry around

Computer Verbs

A **verb** tells an action or what a subject is or does. The following verbs are introduced in this chapter:

VERB	MEANING	EXAMPLE
1. **Turn on**	To give power to the computer so that it works	*Please* **turn on** *the CPU and the monitor so that we can do our work.*

NOTE! Two-word verbs, like *turn on* can have different meanings from just one of the words, like *turn*.

2. **Turn off**	To stop the power from going to the computer	*I am finished with my work, so I can* **turn off** *the computer now.*
3. **Press**	To push a button with your finger	*If you want to turn on the computer, you have to* **press** *the power button.*
4. **Let go**	To take your finger off the mouse button after you press it	*When you use the mouse button, you have to press it and then* **let go.**
5. **Click**	To press and let go of the mouse button in one smooth motion	*Normally, you* **click** *the left mouse button if you want to do something on the computer.*
6. **Go to**	To move your mouse pointer to an icon or program name that you see on your screen	*If you want to practice dragging, you can use the mouse to* **go to** *different icons and drag them on the screen.*
7. **Select**	To choose a letter, word, sentence, paragraph, or program	*I want to move that icon, so I will* **select** *and then drag it.*
8. **Shut down**	To turn off the computer using the Start menu	*I am finished with my work, so I will* **shut down** *the computer.*
9. **Drag**	To use your mouse to move something to a different place on the screen	*I don't like that icon in that corner, so I will* **drag** *it to a different place.*

NOTE! In this chapter, the verb form *dragging* may be used instead of the verb form *drag*.

Concepts and Exercises

How We Use Computers

Computers are an important part of life today, so it is important to learn how to use them. Computers can be very useful at home and at work.

Here are some common things that you can learn to do with a computer:

- Apply for a job

- Type a letter

- Make a picture or graph

- Find maps and driving directions

- Find information that you need for school or work reports

- Send and receive mail, even from other countries

- Translate words

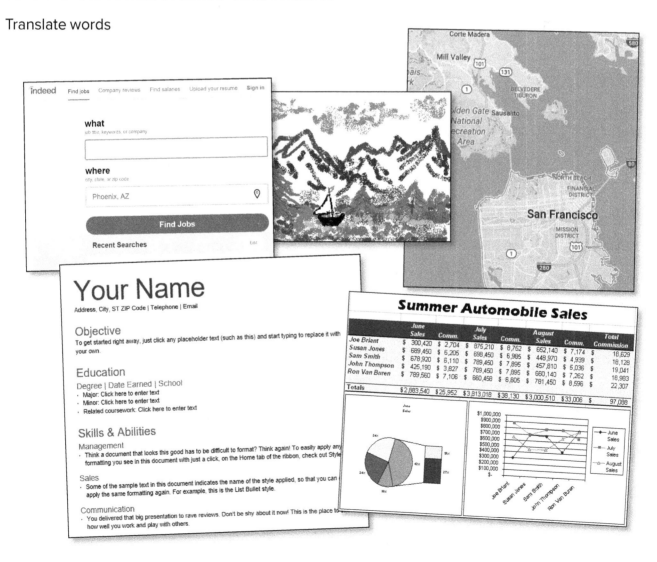

Parts of the Computer

Here are the parts of a computer system. Each one has its own job.

A **CPU** – The CPU (central processing unit) is where all the "thinking" is done. Some people call it a tower. CPUs come in different shapes and sizes.

B **Monitor** – The CPU uses the monitor to give you information. It shows you what the computer is doing.

C **Speakers** – The speakers let you hear the sounds that the computer makes.

D **Keyboard** – You use the keyboard to type numbers and letters into the computer.

E **Mouse** – The mouse lets you point at and select different things on the computer screen.

▶ EXERCISE 1.1

In this exercise, you will find the parts of the computer.

1. Sit down at a computer.

2. Look at the picture of the parts of the computer above. Find those parts on your computer.

The Correct Way to Sit at the Computer

It is important to sit correctly when using the computer so that your body will not hurt after using it.

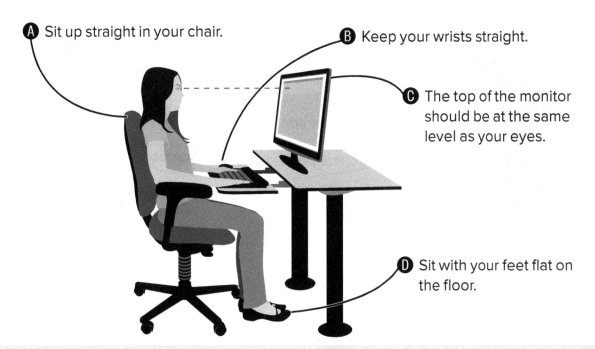

A Sit up straight in your chair.

B Keep your wrists straight.

C The top of the monitor should be at the same level as your eyes.

D Sit with your feet flat on the floor.

The correct way to sit at a computer

▶ EXERCISE 1.2

In this exercise, you will sit at the computer in the correct way.

1. Sit in a chair in front of a computer. Put your hands on the keyboard.

2. You should have your feet, back, wrists, and eyes in the correct positions.

Turning On the Computer

On the front of the CPU, you will see some slots and buttons. Each one has a job.

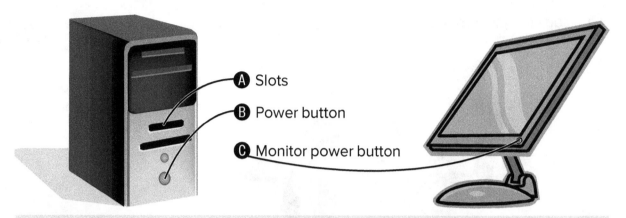

(A) Slots

(B) Power button

(C) Monitor power button

To turn on the computer, press the CPU power button. To turn on the screen, press the monitor power button.

▶ EXERCISE 1.3

In this exercise, you will turn on the computer and monitor.

1. Push the **power** button on the CPU of the computer.

2. Listen for the computer to turn on. You may hear a beep or other noise as it warms up.

3. Push the **power** button on the monitor to turn it on.

Once the computer and monitor have been on for a few minutes, you should see the Windows Desktop.

What Is Windows?

Windows is a program that you can use to communicate with the CPU. Before you can use the computer, Windows must be put onto it. The CPU uses Windows to communicate in a language that you can understand. It also tells the other programs and machines that are attached to the computer, such as the printer, what to do.

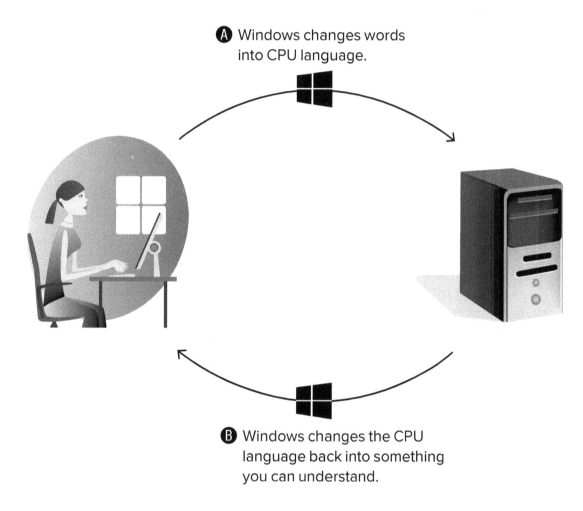

Ⓐ Windows changes words into CPU language.

Ⓑ Windows changes the CPU language back into something you can understand.

In this book, we will use Windows 10.

▶ EXERCISE 1.4

In this exercise, you will move the mouse on the Windows Desktop.

1. Look at the Windows Desktop on the screen. It should look similar to the screen below. (It may have a different picture on it or none at all.)

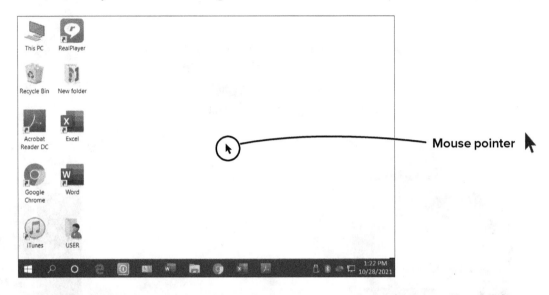

2. Move your mouse around and watch the mouse pointer (the small arrow) move on the screen.

Using a Mouse

You can use the mouse to point at things on the screen. It is called a mouse because the cord looks like a tail. Some mice come without cords and are called cordless mice.

When using the mouse, remember these tips:

- You usually use the left button of the mouse to click.

- If you need to use the right button, you will be told to right-click.

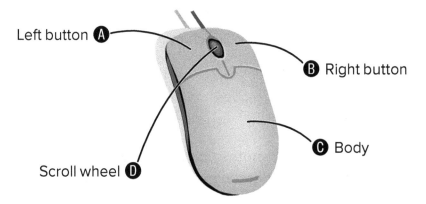

Left button Ⓐ

Ⓑ Right button

Ⓒ Body

Scroll wheel Ⓓ

- You use your thumb and your fourth finger to hold the mouse and move it to new places.

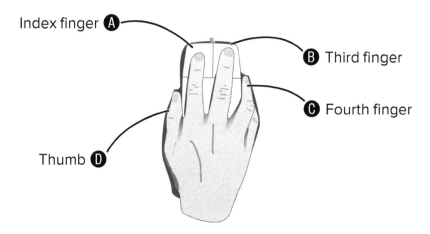

Index finger Ⓐ

Ⓑ Third finger

Ⓒ Fourth finger

Thumb Ⓓ

▶ EXERCISE 1.5

In this exercise, you will use the mouse to move icons around the Desktop.

1. Hold the sides of the mouse with your thumb and fourth finger. You should have one finger on each button. Do not hold it too tightly!

2. Put the bottom part of your hand on the mouse pad or desk.

3. Move the mouse around and watch the mouse pointer move on the screen.

4. Move the mouse so the pointer is on top of an icon on the Desktop. Click (press and let go) the left mouse button one time and see the color change on the icon.

   This is how the icon should look after you click it.

5. Move your mouse to put the pointer on top of another icon. Hold down the left button and move the mouse. You should see the icon move to a new place when you let go. This is called dragging.

6. Practice dragging icons to different parts of the Desktop.

. . . .

Turning Off the Computer

To keep the computer working correctly, you must turn it off correctly.

Start→Power→Shut Down

This is an example of a command. When you give a command, you tell the computer to do a task for you.

▶ EXERCISE 1.6

In this exercise, you will turn off the computer.

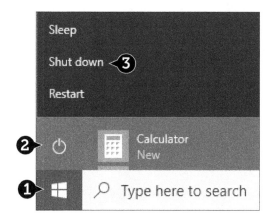

1. Click the **Start** button.

2. Move the mouse pointer up and click **Power**.

3. Click **Shut Down**.

   Do not push the power button on the CPU. It will go off by itself.

⟨⚊⚊⟩ Skill Builder Exercises

▶ SKILL BUILDER 1.1 **Turn On the Computer**

In this exercise, you will turn on the computer and monitor.

1. Press the **power** button on the CPU. The computer may make a beep or other noise.

2. Press the **power** button on the monitor to turn it on if it is not already on.

▶ SKILL BUILDER 1.2 **Drag Icons**

In this exercise, you will **drag icons on the screen.**

1. Use your mouse to drag some of the icons on the Desktop to the bottom-right corner of the screen.

2. Use your mouse to drag some of the icons on the Desktop to the top-right corner of the screen.

3. Use your mouse to drag some of the icons on the Desktop to the left side of the screen.

▶ SKILL BUILDER 1.3 **Turn Off the Computer**

In this exercise, you will turn off the computer and monitor.

1. Click the **Start** button.

2. Move the mouse pointer up, click **Power**, and then click **Shut Down**.

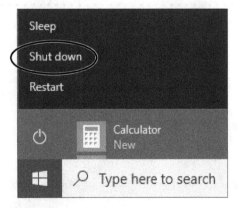

3. Press the **power** button on the monitor to turn it off.

   Do not push the power button on the CPU. It will go off by itself.

▶ SKILL BUILDER 1.4 **Describe Computer Parts**

In this exercise, you will describe the different parts of the computer.

1. On a piece of paper, draw a picture of at least four parts of a computer system.

2. Write in your own words how each part looks.

3. On a piece of paper, draw a picture of a laptop. Write a sentence about how a laptop is different from a regular computer.

· ·

# Paired Conversation

With a partner, take turns reading the A and B parts of the conversation.

Partner A	Hi. What is that?
Partner B	This is my new computer.
Partner A	Really? How exciting!
Partner B	Let me show you. This is the CPU.
Partner A	I know. It is the brain.
Partner B	That is right! This is the monitor.
Partner A	Wow! It has a nice screen.
Partner B	Yes, it helps me to see what is happening on the computer. Look at my fancy keyboard.
Partner A	I know about the keyboard. My brother takes keyboarding at school.
Partner B	This is the mouse and these are the mouse buttons. The left one is used more than the right.
Partner A	What a cute mouse. Can I push a button?
Partner B	No, not yet! You have to turn on the computer first.
Partner A	Okay. Can I push the power button to turn it on now?
Partner B	Sure. The first thing you see is the Desktop.
Partner A	The screen looks colorful.
Partner B	Thanks. I love my new computer!
Partner A	You are so lucky!

(Q) Chapter Review

1.1 Fill in the Blanks

Using the words in the Word Bank below, label each part of the figure.

WORD BANK

Speakers	Keyboard	Monitor
CPU	Mouse	

1. _____

2. _____

3. _____

4. _____

5. _____

1.2　Verb Worksheet

Fill in the blanks. Select the best answer for each sentence using the computer verbs in the Word Bank.

WORD BANK		
turn on	turn off	go to
press	let go	shut down
click	drag	select

1. To _____ _____ the computer means to turn it off using the Start menu.

2. Before you can use a computer, you must _____ _____ the CPU and the monitor.

3. To press and let go of the mouse button in one smooth motion is called to _____ .

4. To _____ _____ means to take your finger off the mouse button after you press it.

5. When you choose something in particular, you _____ it.

6. To turn on your computer, you have to _____ the power button.

7. When you are finished using the computer, you should _____ _____ the computer.

8. When you want to move something to a different position on the screen, you can _____ it with your mouse.

9. To _____ _____ means to take your mouse pointer to a place on your screen.

1.3 Fill in the Blanks

Write a word in each blank that goes with what the line is pointing to.

1. Sit up _____ in your chair.

2. Keep your _____ straight.

3. The top of the monitor should be at the same level as your _____.

4. Sit with your _____ flat on the floor.

CHAPTER 2

Windows and the Start Menu

Computer Objectives

- Identify the parts of a program window
- Use the Start menu to open a program
- Move a window using the mouse
- Minimize, maximize, restore, and close a window

Language Objectives

- Talk with a partner about the different parts of a window
- Talk about how to find and use different buttons, bars, menus, and the Ribbon
- Describe how to move a window and use the sizing buttons

Learning Resources: **boostyourskills.lablearning.com**

 Vocabulary

Picture Dictionary – Nouns

A **noun** is the name of a person, place, or thing. The following nouns are introduced in this chapter:

1. **Window** – A rectangular area on the screen that shows a program or message

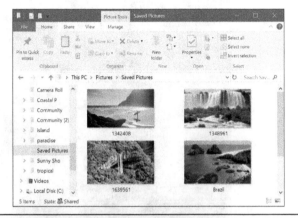

2. **Start menu** – The list that appears when you click the Start button; it shows the main programs

3. **Start button** – The button on the bottom-left corner of your screen that opens the Start menu

4. **Program** – A set of directions (such as computer games, Word, Calculator, and Google Chrome) that tells the computer what to do to get a job done

5. **Minimize button** – The button that looks like a minus sign at the top-right corner of a window; it makes the window disappear, but the program is still open

6. **Maximize button –** The square button between Minimize and Close that makes a window fill the whole screen

7. **Restore button –** The button in the same place as Maximize that changes a large window to a smaller size

8. **Close button –** The button with an "X" that closes the window; it makes the window disappear and closes the program. In Word, the Close button turns red when you put your mouse pointer over it.

9. **Taskbar –** The bar at the bottom of the screen that shows all open programs

10. **Scroll bar –** The bar that lets you move around on the Start menu and other places in Windows; it can be on the side or on the bottom of the Start menu or program you are using

11. **Title bar –** The bar at the top of a window that shows the name of the program you are using

Document1 - Word

12. **Ribbon –** A bar showing different icons; each icon does a different job when you click it

13. **Buttons –** Icons that do different jobs when you click them with the mouse

NOTE! The words *buttons* and *icons* refer to the same thing. Most people call them buttons if they do things when they are clicked with the mouse.

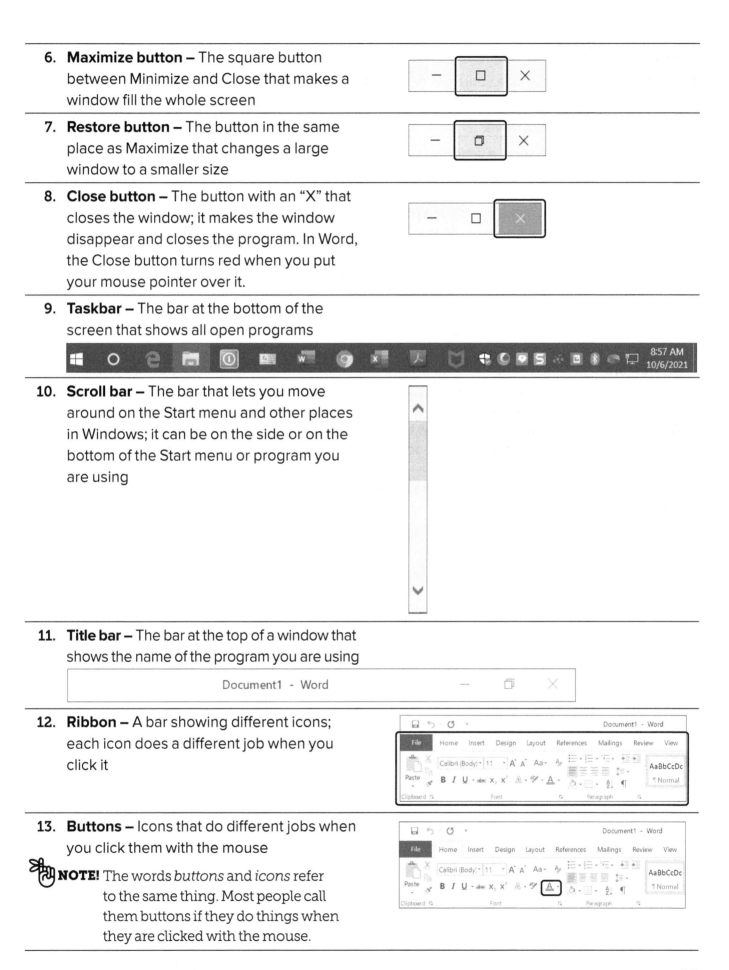

Computer Verbs

A **verb** tells an action or what a subject is or does. The following verbs are introduced in this chapter:

VERB	MEANING	EXAMPLE
1. **Open**	To show a window	*If you want to use Word, you have to* **open** *it first.*
2. **Point**	To make the mouse pointer touch something that you want to choose	*When you want to select an icon, you must first* **point** *to it with your mouse pointer.*
3. **Minimize**	To make a window disappear (but not close) so only its button shows on the taskbar	*I want to* **minimize** *this window so I can look at another window.*
4. **Restore**	To change a maximized window to a smaller size	*I'm going to* **restore** *this window because I do not want it to be so big.*
5. **Maximize**	To make the window larger so that it fills the entire screen	*I need to* **maximize** *my window because I want it to be as big as possible.*
6. **Close**	To stop a program and make it not show on your screen anymore	*Class is finished. Please* **close** *your windows and shut down your computers.*

Concepts and Exercises

The Windows Desktop

The Windows Desktop appears when you turn on the computer. Sometimes it shows a picture. It has these main parts:

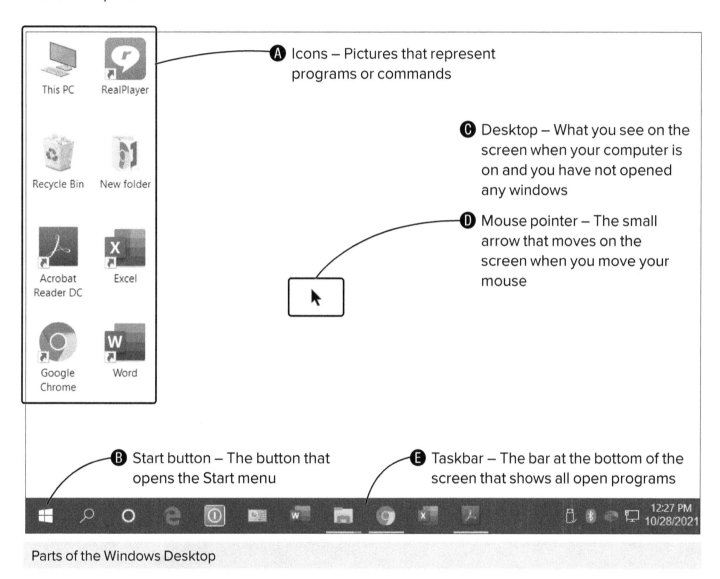

A Icons – Pictures that represent programs or commands

C Desktop – What you see on the screen when your computer is on and you have not opened any windows

D Mouse pointer – The small arrow that moves on the screen when you move your mouse

B Start button – The button that opens the Start menu

E Taskbar – The bar at the bottom of the screen that shows all open programs

Parts of the Windows Desktop

NOTE! You can choose some the icons that appear on the taskbar. Others must appear. Also, the look of an icon may change when the program is updated. For example, the Edge icon (the "e" in the picture above) may look different on your taskbar.

In this exercise, you will use the Windows Desktop.

1. If necessary, turn on the computer.

   The Windows Desktop appears.

2. Move your mouse and watch the mouse pointer move on the screen.

3. Point (do not click) with your mouse pointer over the Recycle Bin.

4. Point (do not click) with your mouse pointer over the Start ⊞ button.

5. Point (do not click) with your mouse pointer over the taskbar.

Opening Programs

You use the Start ⊞ button to start programs with the Start menu. The Start menu shows the programs that the computer can run. The Start menu also allows you to do other tasks, such as turn off the computer.

Scroll Bars

When you do not see what you are looking for on your screen, you can use a scroll bar to move around. Sometimes you have to move your mouse around until you see a scroll bar. They can come in different colors and can show in different places.

Every scroll bar has three parts:

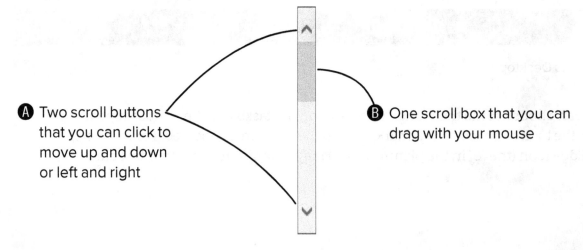

Ⓐ Two scroll buttons that you can click to move up and down or left and right

Ⓑ One scroll box that you can drag with your mouse

▶ EXERCISE 2.2

In this exercise, you will use the Start button to start the Word program.

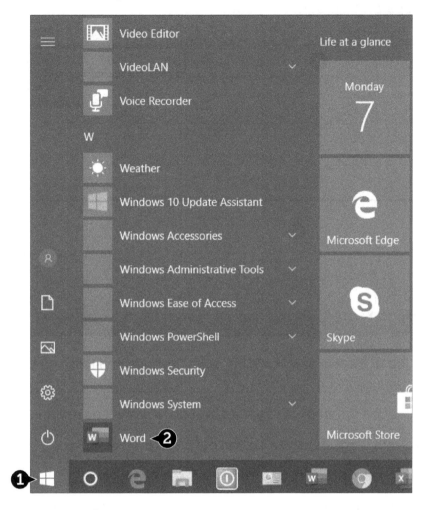

1. Click the **Start** button.

2. Use the scroll bar to move down to the "W" section and then click **Word**.

   There are different versions of Word. If you see Word 2013, Word 2016, or a different version, click that instead.

3. Click **Blank Document**. Leave the Word window open.

Parts of a Program Window

Most program windows have parts similar to what you see on the screen in Word. Look at the picture below to identify the different parts of a program window.

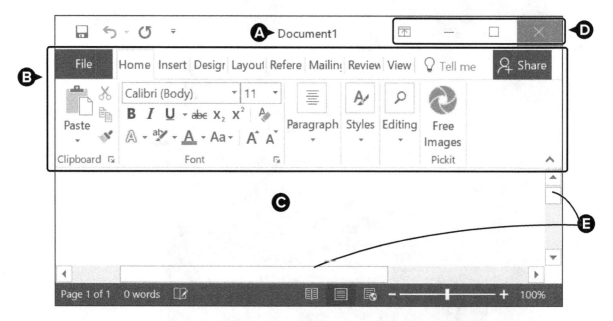

A **Title bar** – This bar at the top of the window holds the sizing buttons and tells you the name of the file you are using.

B **Ribbon** – When you click Ribbon buttons with the mouse, you make things happen on the screen.

C **Work area** – This is where your work shows when you put it into the computer.

D **Window-sizing buttons** – These buttons control the size of the window.

E **Scroll bars** – Help you move around in program windows and on the Start menu. It can be on the side or on the bottom of the screen.

Window-Sizing Buttons

Window-sizing buttons can change the size of the program window, close it, or make it disappear from the screen without closing it.

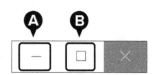

A **Minimize** – This button makes the window disappear when you click on it. The window is not closed, just hiding. To show that window again, click its button on the taskbar.

B **Maximize** – When you click this button, the window fills the whole screen. The Maximize button changes to the Restore button when the window fills the full screen.

C **Restore** – Use this button to return a window to the size it was before it was maximized.

D **Close** – This button closes the window and the program.

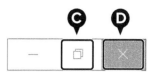

▶ EXERCISE 2.3

In this exercise, you will look at features of the Word program window and use the window-sizing buttons.

NOTE! Do not click in steps 1–5; just point at the parts of the Word window.

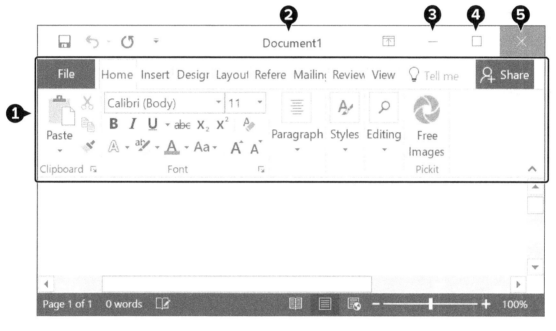

1. Put your mouse pointer on the Ribbon (do not click).

2. Put your mouse pointer on the title bar.

3. Put your mouse pointer on the Minimize ⊟ button.

4. Put your mouse pointer on the Maximize ⊡ button.

5. Put your mouse pointer on the Close ⊠ button.

6. Make the Word window disappear by clicking the **Minimize** ⊟ button.

   Look at the bottom of the screen. You will see a Word button on the taskbar. You did not close Word—you just hid the window.

7. Click the **Word** button on the taskbar to make that window show again.

8. Click the **Maximize** ▫ button to make Word fill the whole screen.

9. Click the **Restore** ▫ button to make the Word window smaller.

10. Click the **Close** ✕ button to close Word.

. . . .

Moving a Window

Sometimes you will want to move a window to see all of it better or to see something behind it.

HOW TO MOVE A WINDOW

A. If the window is already maximized, click the Restore ▫ button. You cannot move a window if it is maximized to fill the whole screen.

B. Put your mouse pointer on the title bar of the window.

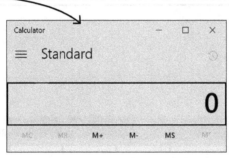

C. Hold down the left mouse button and move the mouse. You can move the window in any direction.

▶ EXERCISE 2.4

In this exercise, you will open the Calculator program and move its program window.

1. Open the Calculator program: **Start→Calculator**

   You may have to use the scroll bar to look down the Start menu to find the Calculator.

2. Put your mouse pointer on the title bar.

3. Hold down the left mouse button and move the calculator window up. Don't drag it up to the top of the screen or you will maximize the Calculator. If that happens, click the **Restore** button.

Press and continue to hold down the left mouse button. Do not release as you do when you click.

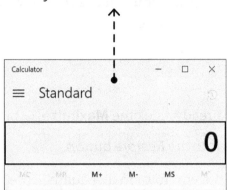

4. Release the mouse button.

5. Hold down the mouse button while it is on the title bar and keep it held down as you drag to the left. Then let go of the mouse button.

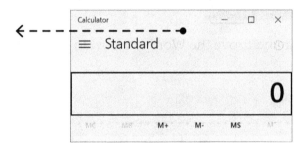

6. Hold down the mouse button and drag to the right. Then let go of the mouse button.

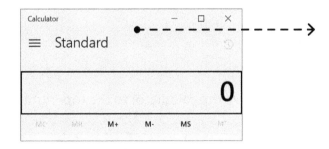

7. Hold down the mouse button and drag down. Let go of the mouse button.

8. Close the Calculator using the **Close** button.

⊕ Skill Builder Exercises

▶ SKILL BUILDER 2.1 **Open and Move the Word Window**

In this exercise, you will open the Word program. You will use the window-sizing buttons and move the Word window around the screen.

1. Open Word: **Start→Word** and click **Blank Document**.

2. Find the title bar and the Ribbon.

3. If the window is not filling the screen already, click the **Maximize** ☐ button.

   Notice that the Maximize button turns into the Restore button.

4. Click the **Restore** ⧉ button to make the window smaller again.

5. Click the **Minimize** – button.

6. Click the **Word** button on the taskbar to restore the window.

7. Put your mouse pointer on the title bar and move the Word window to different places on the screen.

8. Click the **Close** ▨ button to close Word.

▶ SKILL BUILDER 2.2 **Open and Move the Calculator Window**

In this exercise, you will open the Calculator program and move the window around the screen.

1. Open Calculator: **Start→Calculator**

2. Put your mouse pointer on the title bar.

3. Hold down the mouse button and move the calculator to the top-right corner of the screen. Release the mouse button.

4. Move the calculator to the bottom-right corner of the screen.

5. Move the calculator to the top-left corner of the screen.

6. Move the calculator to the bottom-left corner of the Desktop.

7. Move the calculator to the center of the Desktop.

8. **Close** ▨ the Calculator program.

 Paired Conversation

With a partner, take turns reading the A and B parts of the conversation.

Partner A	Good morning.
Partner B	Hi. What are we studying today?
Partner A	I think we are going to learn how to open and close a window.
Partner B	Do our computers have windows?
Partner A	Yes, they can show different programs or a message.
Partner B	Do they appear on the screen?
Partner A	Yes. There are many windows inside your computer.
Partner B	Oh! How do you open a window?
Partner A	Well, we will learn that today.
Partner B	Will we have to use the Start button?
Partner A	Yes, and the Start menu, too.
Partner B	What are the names of some of the programs that you can see in Windows?
Partner A	Word, Calculator, and Google Chrome, so we can use the Internet.
Partner B	I know about the title bar and how to use the Minimize, Maximize, and Restore buttons.
Partner A	That is great. You will learn about the menu bar and the Ribbon, too.
Partner B	What else is important to learn?
Partner A	Well, you should know how to move a window around on the screen.
Partner B	I cannot wait to start!

⊕ Chapter Review

▶ 2.1   Fill in the Blanks

Write the correct name of each part of the Windows Desktop.

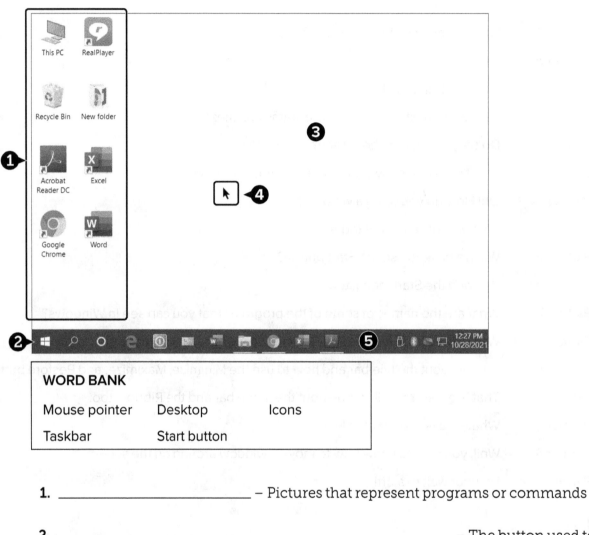

WORD BANK

Mouse pointer	Desktop	Icons
Taskbar	Start button	

1. _____ – Pictures that represent programs or commands

2. _____ _____ – The button used to open the Start menu

3. _____ – The first thing you see on your screen when your computer is turned on and you have not opened any windows

4. _____ _____ – A small object that moves on the screen when you move your mouse

5. _____ – The bar at the bottom of the screen that shows all open programs

▶ 2.2 Fill in the Blanks

Exercise A

Write the name of each item that the arrow is pointing to in the Word window.

WORD BANK

Ribbon	Close	Maximize
Work area	Title bar	Minimize

1. _____

2. _____

3. _____

4. _____

5. _____

6. _____

Exercise B

On a separate piece of paper, write at least four questions using the words from the Word Bank above.

▶ 2.3 Fill in the Blanks

Look at the directions below for opening and sizing the Word window. You have already done this exercise in Skill Builder 2.1. Fill in the blanks to properly open and close the Word window.

1. Open Word: Click _____, then _____. Click Blank Document.

2. Find the title bar.

3. On the top right side of the Word title bar, find the _____, _____, and _____ buttons.

4. Click the _____ button to make the Word window fill the screen. It turns into the _____ button.

5. Click the Restore button to make the window smaller again.

6. Click the _____ button to make the window disappear but not close.

7. Click the _____ button on the taskbar to restore the window.

8. Put your mouse pointer on the _____ to move the Word window to different places on the Desktop.

· ·

CHAPTER 3

Windows Programs

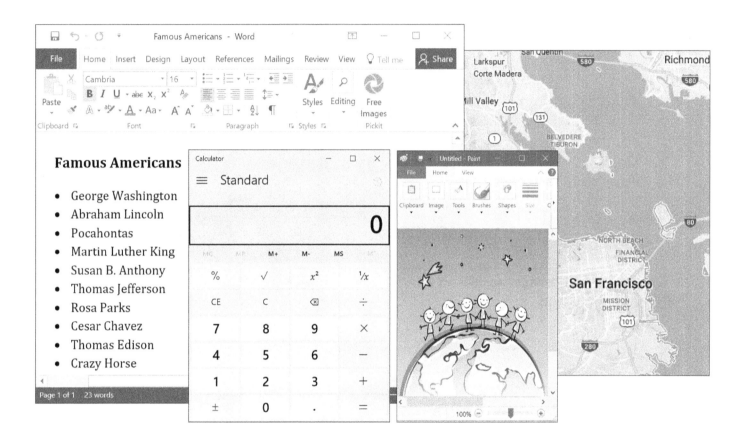

Computer Objectives

■ Use computer hardware and software

■ Use a program Ribbon

■ Open a dialog box and work with a drop-down list

■ Draw a picture in the Paint program

■ Use the Calculator program

■ Play a computer game

Language Objectives

■ Use vocabulary words to describe parts of different programs

■ Use computer verbs to describe actions you can do with different programs

■ Talk with a partner about drawing a picture in the Paint program

■ Talk with a partner about the different kinds of tasks you can do with programs

Learning Resources: **boostyourskills.lablearning.com**

 Vocabulary

Picture Dictionary — Nouns

A **noun** is the name of a person, place, or thing. The following nouns are introduced in this chapter:

1. **Dialog box** – A window with boxes you can click to select what you want

2. **Checkbox** – A box you can click to select an option you want

3. **Drop-down list arrow** – An arrow you can click to make the drop-down list menu appear

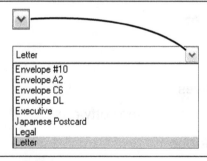

4. **Drop-down list menu** – A list with options you can choose from

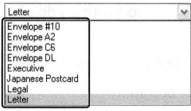

5. **Hardware** – The physical parts of the computer system, such as the monitor or the keyboard

6. **Software** – Programs added to the computer system that are not hardware, such as Word

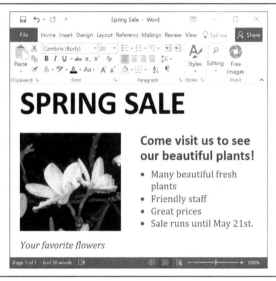

7. **Appearance** – The way an object looks, such as on the computer screen

✋**NOTE!** The word *appearance* is a noun. The word *appear* is a verb.

8. **Settings** – Information about how a program is set up

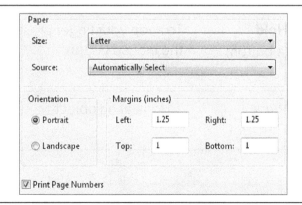

9. **Menu button** – The button you click to open a menu. There are different ways that a menu button can look.

Computer Verbs

A **verb** tells an action or what a subject is or does. The following verbs are introduced in this chapter:

VERB	MEANING	EXAMPLE
1. **Appear**	When an object shows and you can see it	*When you click the box, a checkmark will **appear** inside the box.*
2. **Check**	To click a box so that a checkmark appears	*When you have a few choices, you must **check** the one that you want.*
3. **Clear** (a box)	To click a button or box to remove what you checked before; to uncheck a box	*I changed my mind, so I have to **clear** the box that I checked before.*
4. **Release** (a button)	To take your finger off the mouse button	*After you finish your mouse action, you should **release** the mouse button.*
5. **Let up**	To release or let go of the button	*Another way to say "release the mouse button" is to say "**let up** on the mouse button."*

NOTE! *Release* and *let up* are synonyms. *Synonyms* are words that have the same or a similar meaning.

VERB	MEANING	EXAMPLE
6. **Play**	To use a computer game	*I like to **play** Solitaire and other card games on my computer.*
7. **Preview**	To see how information will look when it is printed so you can decide what you want to do	*I want to **preview** how the document will look before I print it.*
8. **Hold** (a button)	To keep your finger pressed on the mouse button	*Sometimes you have to **hold** down your mouse button for a few seconds, and sometimes you only have to tap it.*
9. **View**	To look at an object	*It is important to **view** the tools on the toolbar so you can see the choices.*

Concepts and Exercises

Common Features in Programs

A program is a set of directions that tells the computer exactly what to do to get a certain kind of job done. Not all programs look the same.

Here are examples of kinds of programs that do different jobs.

A *word-processing program* is used to type text.

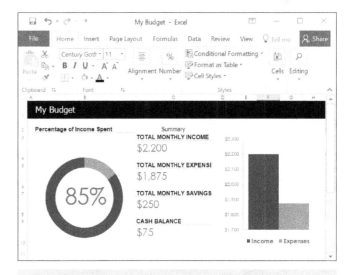

A *spreadsheet program* is used mostly for numbers.

A *graphics program* is used to make and change pictures.

A *web browser* is used to find things on the Internet.

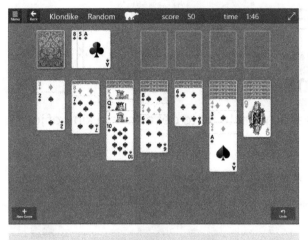

A *computer game* is used to relax and have fun.

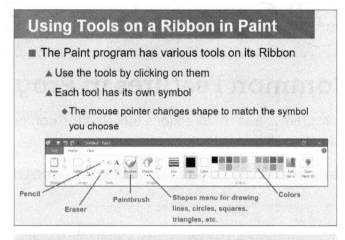

Using Tools on a Ribbon in Paint

■ The Paint program has various tools on its Ribbon

▲ Use the tools by clicking on them

▲ Each tool has its own symbol

◆ The mouse pointer changes shape to match the symbol you choose

A *tutorial* is used to show and teach ideas.

Different programs have many parts that are the same. Most program windows have these parts.

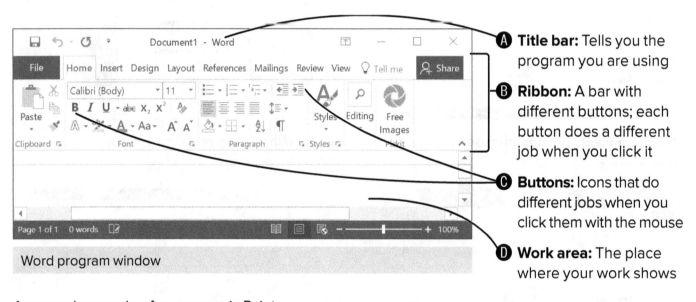

A **Title bar:** Tells you the program you are using

B **Ribbon:** A bar with different buttons; each button does a different job when you click it

C **Buttons:** Icons that do different jobs when you click them with the mouse

D **Work area:** The place where your work shows

Word program window

A second example of a program is Paint.

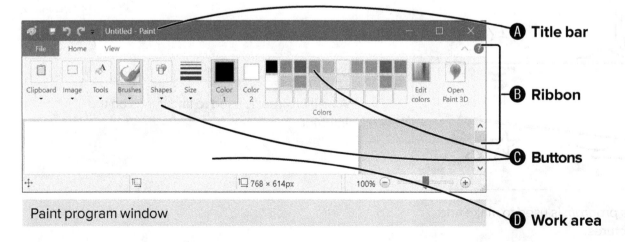

A **Title bar**

B **Ribbon**

C **Buttons**

D **Work area**

Paint program window

▶ EXERCISE 3.1

In this exercise, you will use the Start button to start the Word program. There are different versions of Word. Your computer may show a number after the program name. The recent versions of Word look and function very similarly.

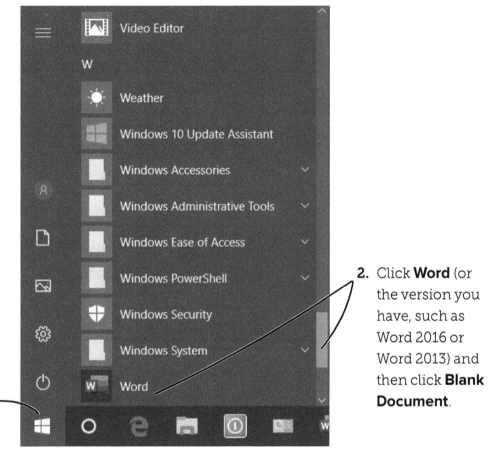

1. Click **Start**.

2. Click **Word** (or the version you have, such as Word 2016 or Word 2013) and then click **Blank Document**.

🔆 **TIP!** You may have to use the scroll bar to move down to the "W" section to see it.

Word opens on the screen.

3. If the Word window does not fill the screen, click the **Maximize** ▢ button.

4. Find the title bar on the screen and point at it with the mouse.

5. Find the Ribbon and the work area. Move your mouse pointer over each part.

Leave Word open for the next exercise.

Dialog Boxes

Most programs have some type of dialog box. You can change settings by changing the information in a dialog box. Many dialog boxes have these features.

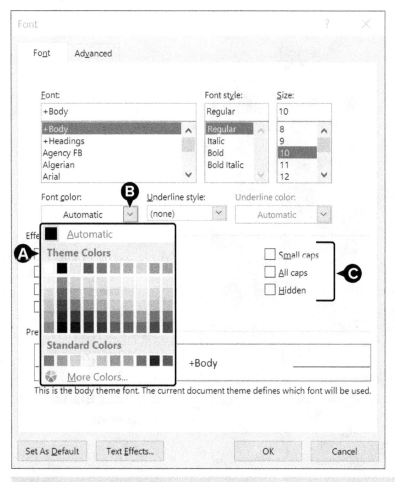

The Word Font dialog box

Ⓐ Drop-down list menu: A list of choices that opens when you click a drop-down arrow.

Ⓑ Drop-down list arrow: An arrow that points down that you can click to open a drop-down list menu.

Ⓒ Checkboxes: Click in the boxes to check or uncheck them.

▶ EXERCISE 3.2

In this exercise, you will use a dialog box in Word. The program should be open from the last exercise.

1. Click the **Home** tab.

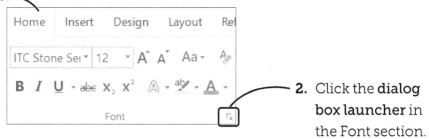

2. Click the **dialog box launcher** in the Font section.

This dialog box will appear on your screen.

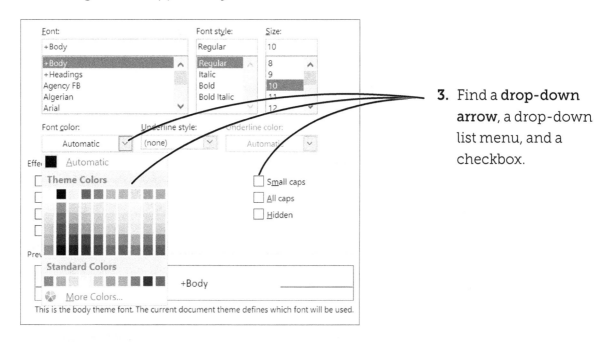

3. Find a **drop-down arrow**, a drop-down list menu, and a checkbox.

4. Click the **Font Color** drop-down arrow to open the drop-down list menu.

5. Close the dialog box with the **Close** ⊠ button. Then, close Word.

Using Ribbon Tools

Paint gives you many tools to work with to make pictures. Some are easy to use, and some take a while to learn. Remember the following when working with tools:

- You can use tools on the Ribbon by clicking the tool buttons.

- When you click a tool button, a symbol appears in place of the mouse pointer. Each tool has its own symbol.

- Tools work only in the white area of the Paint window.

We will not use all of the tools, but here are a few easy ones that show you how they work:

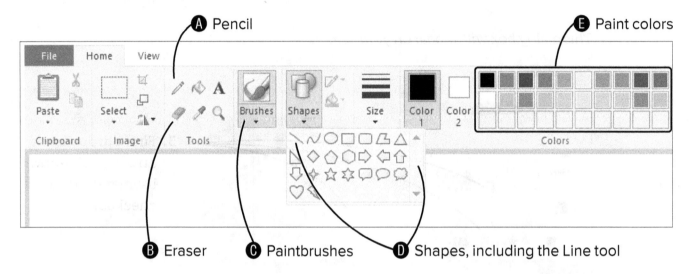

If you want to change the color, click one of the colors on the right side of the Home tab on the Ribbon.

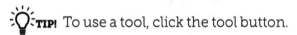 **TIP!** To use a tool, click the tool button.

Paint 3D is another program that comes with Windows. It has even more tools than Paint.

Dragging

To use a tool, you need to drag with the mouse. (For a definition of *drag*, see Chapter 1, "About Computer Basics.") Here is how:

1. Point where you want to start and then hold down your left mouse button.

2. Move the mouse to make your design.

3. Let go of the left mouse button when you are finished making the design.

You will use drag in the next exercise.

▶ EXERCISE 3.3

In this exercise, you will use some of the drawing tools in Paint.

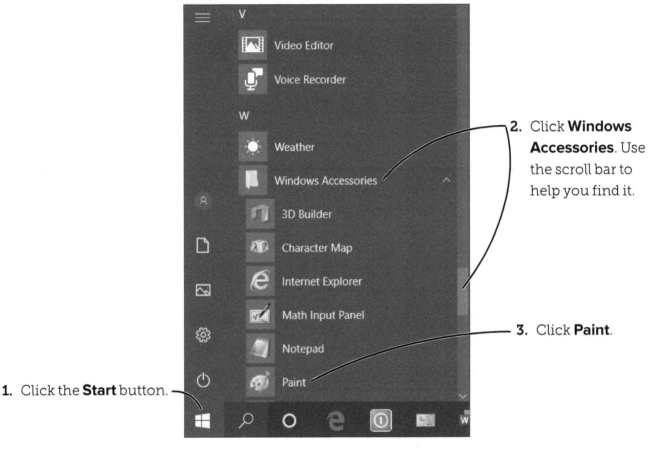

1. Click the **Start** button.

2. Click **Windows Accessories**. Use the scroll bar to help you find it.

3. Click **Paint**.

If necessary, drag the scroll box down until you see Paint.

Draw a Line

4. Maximize ⬜ the Paint window if it does not fill the screen.

5. Locate the **Shapes** group on the Ribbon and choose the **Line** tool from the menu.

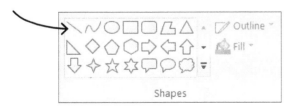

6. Point to a place on the left side of the white area. Hold down your left mouse button and keep it held down until step 8.

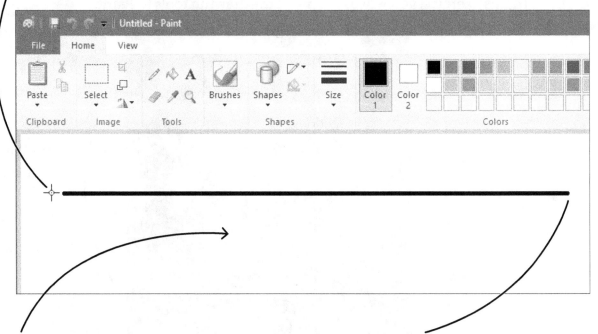

7. Move the mouse to the right. This draws a line.

You should see a line.

8. Let go of the mouse button where you want to stop the line.

Draw a Box

9. In the **Shapes** group, choose the **Rectangle** tool. If the shapes are already showing, just click the shape you want to use.

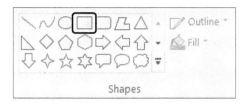

Shapes

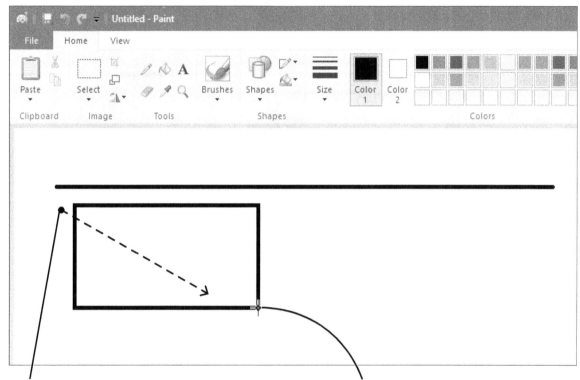

10. Point to a place anywhere on the white area. Hold down the mouse button and move it in the direction shown.

11. Let go of the mouse button.

Draw a Colored Line

12. Click the **Pencil** tool.

13. Click the color **Red** from the Colors box.

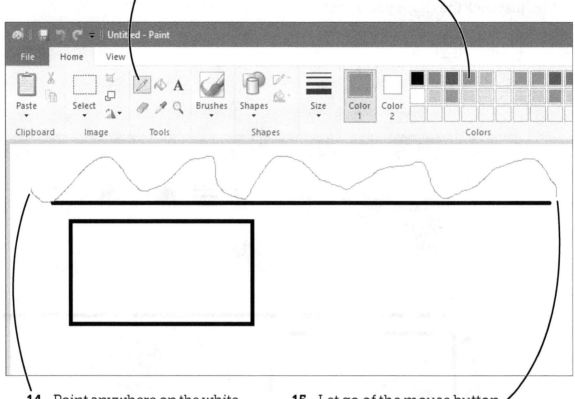

14. Point anywhere on the white area. Hold down the mouse button and then move the mouse up and down and to the right to paint a curving line.

15. Let go of the mouse button.

16. If you make a mistake, you can erase it with the **Eraser** 🖌.

17. You can keep drawing to add anything else you like to your picture.

18. When you are finished, close Paint.

19. If Paint asks you to save your file, click **Don't Save**.

If you already know how to save a file, click Yes and give the file a name.

NOTE! You will learn how to save your files in Chapter 5, "More with Word."

The Windows Calculator

The Calculator is another program on the computer. You can use it to do many calculations. The program looks just like a handheld calculator and works the same way. You can type numbers or you can click the number buttons.

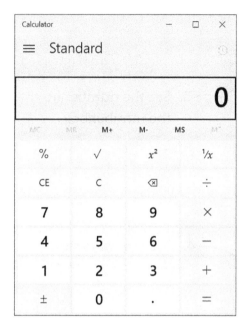

HOW TO USE THE CALCULATOR

Open Calculator: Start→Calculator
Examples of the four basic operations:

Add Two Numbers

   A. Click the first number.

   B. Click the plus (+) sign button.

   C. Click the second number.

   D. Click the equals (=) sign button.

Subtract Two Numbers

   A. Click the first number.

   B. Click the minus (–) sign button.

   C. Click the second number.

   D. Click the equals (=) sign button.

Multiply Two Numbers

Use the multiplication (X) button: (3 X 2 = 6).

Divide Two Numbers

Use the division (÷) button: (8 ÷ 2 = 4).

▶ EXERCISE 3.4

In this exercise, you will use the Calculator to add and subtract. You do not have to type in the numbers. Just click the number buttons with your mouse.

1. Open Calculator: **Start→Calculator**

Add Two Numbers

2. Click the **2** button two times for 22.

3. See the number in the number box.

4. Click the **plus sign** (+) to add the next number.

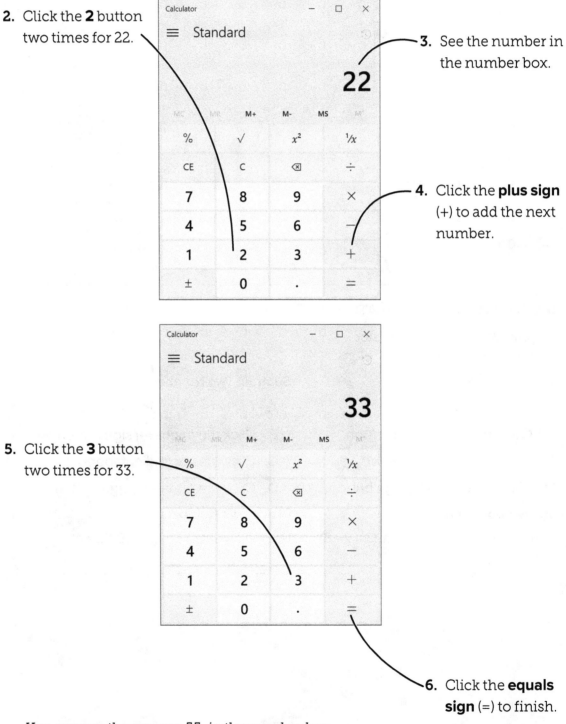

5. Click the **3** button two times for 33.

6. Click the **equals sign** (=) to finish.

You can see the answer, 55, in the number box.

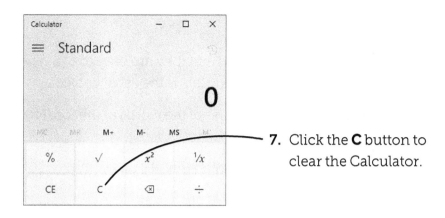

7. Click the **C** button to clear the Calculator.

Do Other Calculations

⚠️ **IMPORTANT** Press C to clear after you complete each of the calculations in steps 8–11.

8. Click these buttons on the calculator: **12 + 6 =**

9. Click these buttons: **100 + 75 =**

10. Click these buttons: **50 – 10 =**

11. Click these buttons: **389 – 14 =**

Leave the Calculator open for the next exercise.

Using Menus

Once you have had some practice using menus, you will find that they are easy to use. The way they work is the same in each program. What changes in each program is the list of choices in the menu.

- You can open a menu by clicking the menu ☰ button or one of the words at the top. Not all programs have menus. Some have only a Ribbon or other buttons.

- Sometimes when you click on one of the menu items, a dialog box will open.

- Sometimes a menu will show on the left side of the window.

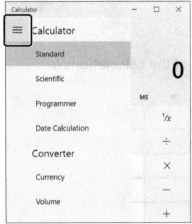 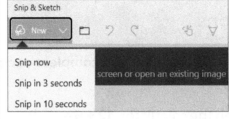 

▶ EXERCISE 3.5

In this exercise, you will use a menu. Many settings can be changed only by using menus.

1. Click the **menu** button.

2. Choose **Scientific**.

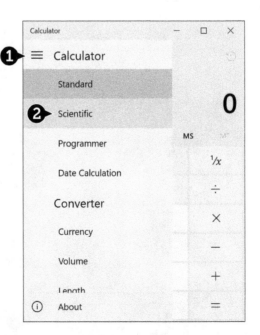

The Calculator now shows the Scientific view with more advanced buttons.

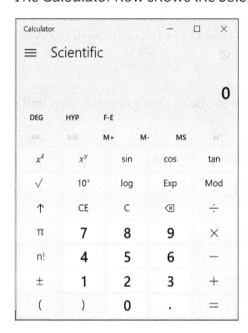

3. Click the **menu** button and then click **Standard** to return the Calculator to normal.

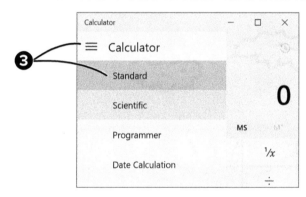

4. Close the Calculator.

(⚙) Skill Builder Exercises

▶ SKILL BUILDER 3.1 **Use Paint**

In earlier exercises, you tried some Paint tools. In this exercise, you will create a real drawing.

1. Open Paint: **Start→Windows Accessories→Paint**

   Use the Start menu scroll bar to go down to Window Accessories and, if necessary, to Paint.

2. Maximize the Paint window.

3. Use some of the tools and colors to draw a picture of a sunset.

   The sunset does not have to look perfect. This is just to practice using the mouse and dragging to draw. Many programs let you do this.

4. When you are finished, close Paint.

5. If Paint asks if you want to save your work, click **Don't Save**.

   If you already know how to save a file, click Yes and give the file a name.

▶ SKILL BUILDER 3.2 **Use the Calculator**

In this exercise, you will use the Calculator program to multiply, divide, and subtract numbers.

1. Open Calculator: **Start→Calculator**

2. To multiply, press these buttons: **3 × 12 =**

3. To multiply, press these buttons: **25 × 2 =**

4. To divide, press these buttons: **80 ÷ 4 =**

5. To divide, press these buttons: **36 ÷ 12 =**

6. To subtract, press these buttons: **99 – 43 =**

7. To subtract, press these buttons: **52 – 12 =**

8. When you are finished, close the Calculator.

▶ SKILL BUILDER 3.3 **Play a Game**

In this exercise, you will play Solitaire. Playing this game will give you good practice using the mouse.

1. Open Solitaire: **Start→Microsoft Solitaire Collection→Classic Solitaire Klondike**

2. Close any windows that may open before you see the game.

3. Click **Play as a Guest**, if necessary.

4. Click **Klondike** and then click **Play**.

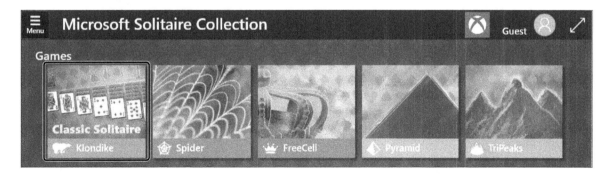

5. To move one of the cards, click on it. Hold down the mouse button and drag it to a new place. If you put a card in the wrong place, it will not stay there. It will jump back to where it was.

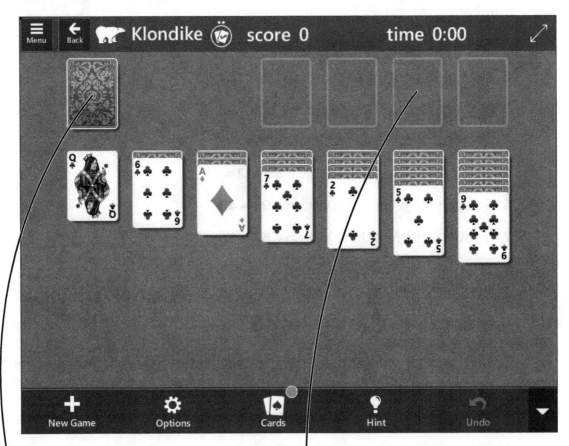

6. When you want to turn over a new card, click on the pack at the top.

7. Start putting the aces in the four shaded areas and build up from there. The suits (pictures on the cards) must match in each top pile. You must put all the cards in the top piles to win.

8. If you want to start a new game, click **New Game** on the bottom-left side of the window.

9. When you are finished playing, click the **Close** button.

▶ SKILL BUILDER 3.4 **Draw a Map**

In this exercise, you will draw and print a simple map with the Paint program.

1. Open Paint: **Start→Windows Accessories→Paint**

2. Draw lines to create a simple street map of the area around your house.

💡**TIP!** To draw straight lines, hold down the [Shift] key as you drag a new line.

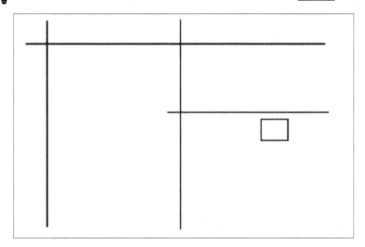

3. Use the **Text A** tool to add street names. Click near where you want to type the words. Hold down the mouse button and drag a text box. Then you can type a street name inside the box. Make a new box for each name. After you type each street name, click outside of that text box before you make a new text box or draw another line.

```
                    Main Street



First Street


                Ponderosa Street


                              ┌──────┐
                              │      │
                              └──────┘
```

4. To print the map, choose **File→Print** and then click **Print** again.

5. Close Paint without saving the map. (Or, if you know how to save a file, use **File→Save As** to save it.)

# Paired Conversation

With a partner, take turns reading the A and B parts of the conversation.

Partner A	Yesterday we learned how to minimize a window.
Partner B	Yes, I remember. The window disappeared but did not really close.
Partner A	Do you remember how to maximize a window?
Partner B	Yes. Now let's talk about what we learned today.
Partner A	Today we learned about hardware.
Partner B	Is that like the computer and the monitor?
Partner A	Right. We also learned about software.
Partner B	That is like Word and Paint that are added into the computer.
Partner A	That is true.
Partner B	We also learned about the dialog boxes.
Partner A	Yes. Dialog boxes are important because they let you select the settings that you want.
Partner B	Did you play a computer game today?
Partner A	Not really. I just watched somebody else play.
Partner B	We practiced using the Paint program.
Partner A	I liked drawing a map and typing the names of the streets.
Partner B	Well, I am so glad we are learning so much!

⊖ Chapter Review

3.1 Verb Worksheet

Fill in the blanks. Select the best answer for each sentence using the computer verbs in the Word Bank.

> **WORD BANK**
>
> | | | |
> |---|---|---|
> | appear | check | clear |
> | let up | play | preview |
> | release | view | hold |

1. You can _____ a document to see how it will look when you print it.

2. To _____ is when an object shows on the screen and you can see it.

3. To uncheck a box is called to _____ it.

4. To _____ a box means to click the box so that a checkmark appears.

5. To look at something is to _____ it.

6. To _____ means to use a computer game.

7. To keep your finger pressed on the mouse button is to _____ the button.

8. To _____ means to take your finger off of the mouse button.

9. To _____ means to release or let go of a button.

3.2　Fill in the Blanks

Fill in the missing words in the sentences below. Look at the picture of the Windows Calculator to help you.

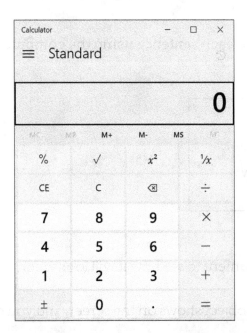

Exercise A: Add Two Numbers

1. Click the first _____.

2. Click the _____ sign.

3. Click the _____.

4. Click the _____ sign.

Exercise B: Multiply Two Numbers

1. Click the first _____.

2. Click the _____ sign.

3. Click the _____.

4. Click the _____ sign.

CHAPTER 4

Creating a Document in Word

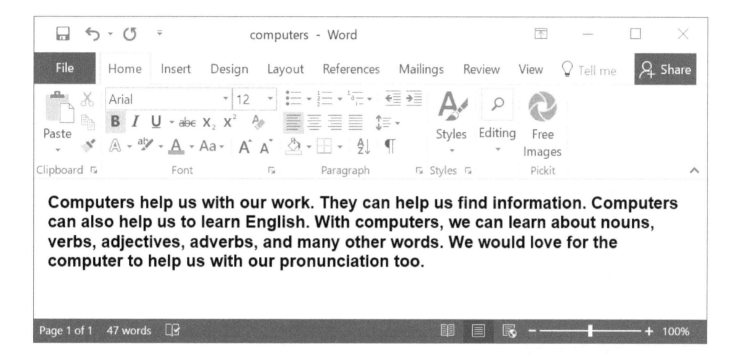

Computer Objectives

- Use the computer keyboard
- Create and edit a Word document
- Print a document

Language Objectives

- Use vocabulary words to discuss using Word and the keyboard
- Use computer verbs to describe how to use Word and the keyboard
- Use computer language to talk about how to create a document

Learning Resources: **boostyourskills.lablearning.com**

 Vocabulary

Picture Dictionary – Nouns

A **noun** is the name of a person, place, or thing. The following nouns are introduced in this chapter:

1. **Cursor** – A line on the screen that shows where you are going to type text

The cursor blinks on and off.

2. **Arrow keys** – Keys that move your cursor to another place without erasing

3. **Backspace key** – A key that erases what is to the left of the cursor

4. **Enter key** – A key that moves the cursor to the next line

5. **Shift key** – A key that helps make a capital letter or the top symbol of a typed key

NOTE! Capital letters are used at the beginning of sentences and for the first letter of names. In English, we also capitalize the first letter of the days of the week and the months of the year, among other words.

6. **Delete key –** A key that erases what is to the right of the cursor

7. **Spacebar –** The bar that puts a space between words

8. **Text –** The letters, numbers, and symbols you type on the keyboard

Aa Bb Cc 1 2 3

9. **Printer –** A machine that puts information from the computer onto a sheet of paper

Computer Verbs

A **verb** tells an action or what a subject is or does. The following verbs are introduced in this chapter:

VERB	MEANING	EXAMPLE
1. **Delete**	To take away or erase	*I typed the wrong word. I will **delete** it and type the correct word.*

NOTE! The words *erase* and *remove* are synonyms of the word *delete*.

VERB	MEANING	EXAMPLE
2. **Type**	To use the keyboard to put text on the page	*I do not know how to **type**, so I have to take a keyboarding class.*
3. **Wrap**	To make words automatically continue onto the next line	*When you type a paragraph, the computer will **wrap** the words onto the next line.*
4. **Insert** (text)	To type text between two other letters or words	*I forgot to type my middle name. I need to **insert** it between my first name and last name.*
5. **Print**	To put a document from your computer onto a sheet of paper	*I finished my letter. Now I will **print** it and mail it to my grandmother.*

Concepts and Exercises

The Computer Keyboard

The computer keyboard has more keys than a typewriter. In this chapter, you will use the most common keys. Here are some important keyboard keys:

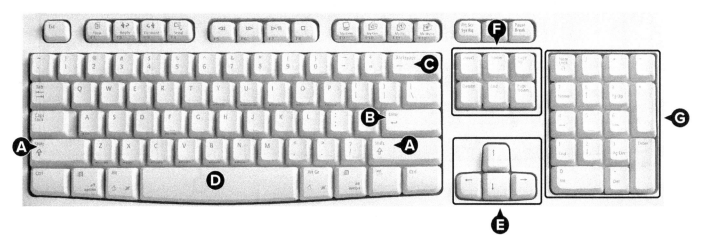

A Shift keys

B Enter key

C Backspace key

D Spacebar

E Arrow keys

F Delete, Home, and other special keys

G Numeric keypad

▶ EXERCISE 4.1

In this exercise, you will find the keys on the computer keyboard.

NOTE! Your keyboard may not look exactly like the one on this page.

1. Look at the computer keyboard.

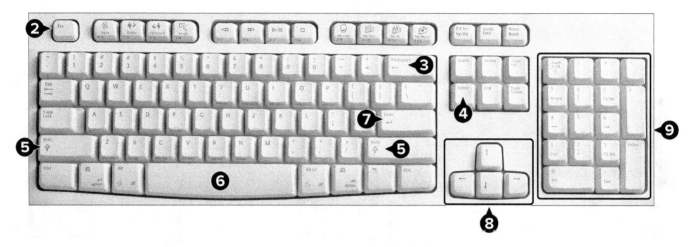

2. Look at the top row of keys. None of them are on a typewriter.

3. Find the [Backspace] key.

4. Find the [Delete] key.

5. Find the [Shift] keys.

6. Find the [Spacebar].

7. Find the [Enter] key.

8. Find the arrow keys.

9. Find the numeric keypad on the right side of the keyboard.

Using the Keyboard

It is important to learn how to type well on a keyboard. The best way is to take a keyboarding class. Your hands should rest on the keyboard like this. Notice that your fingers are resting on the middle row of the letter keys. This is called the *home row*.

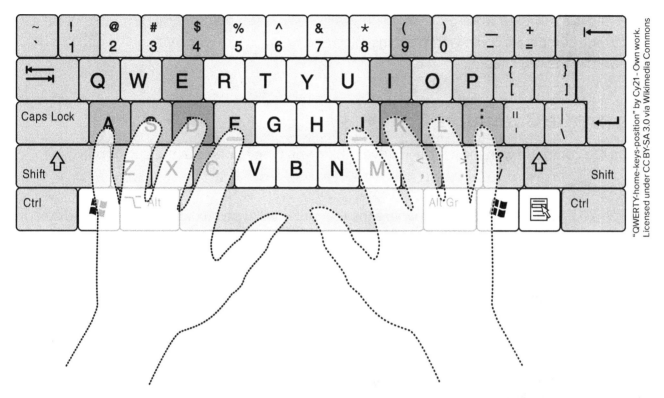

▶ EXERCISE 4.2

In this exercise, you will place your hands on the keyboard.

1. Put your hands on the keyboard with your fingers on the keys as shown above. You should feel a small bump on both the F and J keys.

2. Move your fingers up and down to touch the other keys.

Word-Processing Programs

A word-processing program helps you type on the computer. You can create letters, notes, lists, and many other things. Most computers come with a simple word-processing program. You can also use one on the Internet.

Microsoft Word is a powerful word-processing program that you can buy separately and install on a computer. Some computers come with Word installed and ready to use when you buy them. You used Microsoft Word in the last chapter.

Typing on the Computer

You type on the computer with the keyboard. Everything you type appears at the cursor position.

The Cursor

| The cursor is a blinking line that shows where the computer will type next. You can move the cursor anywhere you have typed. You will learn how to move it soon.

Word Wrap

When you are typing and reach the end of a line, the computer will automatically put the next words you type on the next line for you. That is called *Word Wrap*.

> **Computers help us with our work. They can help us find information. Computers can also help us to learn English. With computers, we can learn about nouns, verbs, adjectives, adverbs, and many other words. We would love for the computer to help us with our pronunciation too.**

This is what a paragraph looks like with Word Wrap.

> **Computers help us with our work. They can help us find information. Computers can also help**

This is how the same text shows without Word Wrap. The other words continue to the right but do not show on the page.

Enter Key

The Enter key starts a new line wherever the cursor is. You only need to use the Enter key at the end of a short line or a paragraph.

Spacebar

The Spacebar is the longest key. You use it to make a space between words.

▶ EXERCISE 4.3

In this exercise, you will type in Word and see how Word Wrap works.

1. Open Word: **Start→Word** (or your version; remember to use the scroll bar to move to the "W" section of the menu). Then, click **Blank Document**.

2. Type the sentences in the paragraph below.

   Do not *press* Enter. *When there is not enough space on the line, the words will go to the next line.*

   ☀ **TIP!** To capitalize a letter, hold down Shift while typing the letter you would like to capitalize.

   ```
   Computers help us with our work. They can help us
   find information. Computers can also help us to learn
   English. With computers, we can learn about nouns, verbs,
   adjectives, adverbs, and many other words. We would love
   for the computer to help us with our pronunciation too.
   ```

   This is how your screen should look when you are finished. Your lines may end at different places. Computers have different settings and may have different line breaks. Don't worry if your lines of text are longer or shorter than what is shown in the picture.

   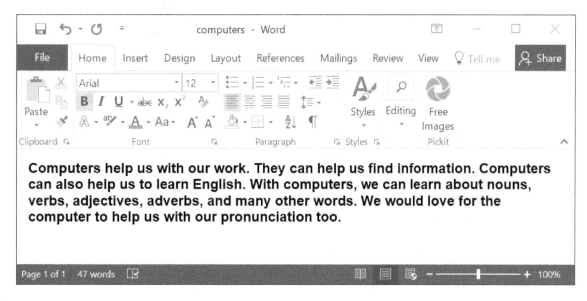

3. Leave this document open for the next exercise.

Inserting Text

You can insert text by moving the cursor and then typing. You must first put the cursor where you want using the mouse or the arrow (cursor) keys. Then when you type, the new letters appear where the cursor is blinking.

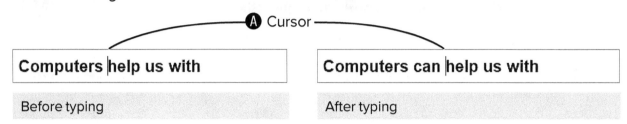

(A) Cursor

| **Computers \|help us with** | **Computers can \|help us with** |
| Before typing | After typing |

Arrow Keys

The arrow keys on the keyboard are also called the cursor keys. Each time you tap an arrow key, the cursor moves once in that direction.

▶ EXERCISE 4.4

In this exercise, you will insert a word and insert new lines into your Word document.

1. Click to the left of the word *help*.

   ❶

   Computers \|help us with our work. They can he

2. Type **can** and press [Spacebar].

   Computers can help us
   ❷

   Now you will make two blank lines.

3. Move your mouse to the left of the *C* in *Computers* at the beginning of the first sentence. Click only when you see the mouse pointer change to this symbol: [I]

   ❸ **\|Computers can help us with our work. They c**
   Computers can also help us to learn English.
   about nouns, verbs, adjectives, adverbs, and

4. Press [Enter] to make a new line.

   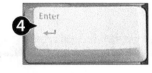

5. Press the **up arrow** key once (to get to the top of the document).

   Now you are ready to type a new line.

6. Type the new line: **Typing in a Word Processor**

> **Typing in a Word Processor**
>
> Computers can help us with our work. Th

It is easy to add new lines or words at any time.

7. Leave this document open for the next exercise.

Deleting Text

You can delete (remove) letters, words, and even entire lines from a word-processing document. There are two ways to do this: by using the Delete key or the Backspace key.

Delete Key

This key deletes letters to the right (→) of the cursor. You remove one letter or space each time you tap the Delete key.

Ⓐ Cursor

> Computers | can help us with our work. T

Before Delete

> Computers |help us with our work. T

After Delete

Backspace Key

This key deletes letters to the left (←) of the cursor. You remove one letter or space each time you tap the Backspace key.

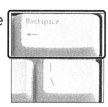

Ⓐ Cursor

> Computers can |help us with

Before Backspace

> Computers |help us with our work. T

After Backspace delete

▶ EXERCISE 4.5

In this exercise, you will delete some words from your document. First you will use the Delete key to delete text to the right of the cursor. Then you will use the Backspace key to delete text to the left of the cursor.

Use the Delete Key

1. Click to the left of the word *can* in the second line of text.

> **Typing in a Word Processor**
>
> Computers |can help us with our work.
>
> ❶

2. Press Delete Delete Delete Delete to erase the word *can* and the space after it.

> **Typing in a Word Processor**
>
> Computers |help us with our work.
>
> ❷

Use the Backspace Key

3. Click to the right of the sentence *They can help us find information.*

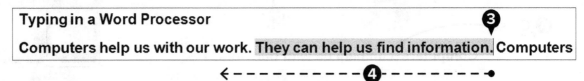

> **Typing in a Word Processor**   ❸
>
> Computers help us with our work. They can help us find information.|Computers
>
> ←– – – – – – – – – ❹ – – – – – – – – •

4. Press Backspace until the whole sentence is gone and then one more time to take out the extra space.

This is what the screen should look like after step 4.

> **Typing in a Word Processor**
>
> Computers help us with our work.|Computers can also help us to learn English.

5. Leave this document open for the next exercise.

Printing Your Work

You will often want to print documents that you type. Some programs have more than one method you can use to give the print command.

Here is how to print in Word:

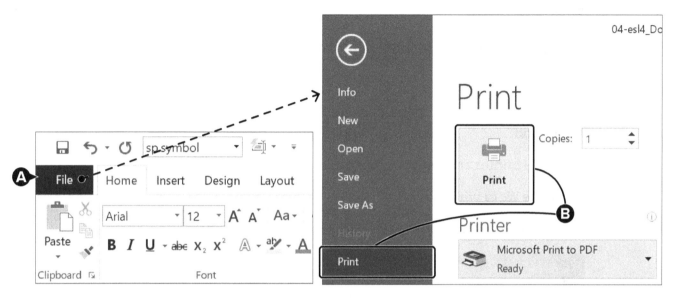

(A) Begin by clicking File at the top-left part of the Ribbon.

(B) Choose Print from the menu and then click the big Print button.

Your computer sends the document to the printer, and the printer puts it onto the paper.

▶ EXERCISE 4.6

In this exercise, you will add your name to your Word file and then print it.

1. Use the arrow keys or the mouse to go to the very bottom of your Word document text.

2. Press ⌐Enter⌐ two times.

3. Type your name at the bottom of the document.

4. Choose **File→Print**.

5. When the Print screen opens, click the **Print** button to finish the command.

6. Go to the printer and get your document.

7. Close the Word window.

Word will ask if you wish to save changes to your document.

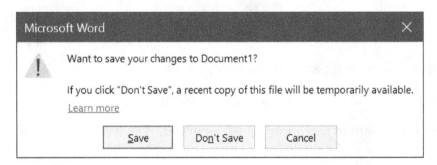

8. Click **Don't Save** to close the Word program without saving your document.

You will learn how to save your documents in Chapter 5, "More with Word."

Skill Builder Exercises

▶ SKILL BUILDER 4.1 **Type Sentences**

In this exercise, you will type a simple document with Word.

1. Open Word: **Start→Word** (or your version) and click **Blank Document**.

2. Type the following sentences.

   Use Shift *to make capital letters. Press* Enter *only where it appears below.*

   The cursor shows where you are going to type text. Enter

   You use a keyboard when you want to put letters or numbers into the computer. Enter

   The Shift key lets you type a capital letter or the top symbol on a key. Enter

   Press the Enter key when you want to start typing text on another line. Enter

   Arrow keys are used to move to another place without erasing. Enter

   Place the cursor to the left of text and press the Delete key to erase. Enter

   Place the cursor to the right of text and press the Backspace key to erase. Enter

3. Choose **File→Print→Print** to print your work.

4. Close Word. Click **Don't Save** when Word asks if you want to save your work.

▶ SKILL BUILDER 4.2 **Type the Punctuation Marks**

In this exercise, you will type a list of punctuation marks with Word. Then you will insert a title for the list.

1. Open Word: **Start→Word** (or your version) and open a new document.

2. Type the following sentences.

   You must use Shift *to type some of the punctuation marks. Press* Enter *only where it appears below.*

   . A period is used at the end of a statement or a command. Enter

   , A comma is used to separate words or phrases. Enter

   : A colon is used to introduce a list. Enter

   ! An exclamation mark is used at the end of a sentence that shows surprise or strong feeling. Enter

   ? A question mark is used at the end of every sentence that asks a question. Enter

   When you finish, your screen should look like this:

   . A period is used at the end of a statement or a command.

   , A comma is used to separate words or phrases.

   : A colon is used to introduce a list.

   ! An exclamation mark is used at the end of a sentence that shows surprise or strong feeling.

   ? A question mark is used at the end of every sentence that asks a question.

Insert a Title for the List

3. Put the cursor at the top left of the list. (Use the arrow keys.)

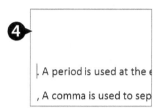

4. Press ⌷Enter⌷ two times.

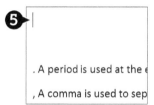

5. Press the up arrow ⌷↑⌷ key two times to move the cursor to the top.

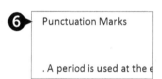

6. Type the title: **Punctuation Marks**

Now your screen should look like this:

Punctuation Marks

. A period is used at the end of a statement or a command.

, A comma is used to separate words or phrases.

: A colon is used to introduce a list.

! An exclamation mark is used at the end of a sentence that shows surprise or strong feeling.

? A question mark is used at the end of every sentence that asks a question.

7. Choose **File→Print→Print** to print your work.

8. Close Word. Click **Don't Save** when Word asks if you wish to save your work.

▶ SKILL BUILDER 4.3 **Type a Paragraph**

In this exercise, you will type a paragraph with Word.

1. Open Word: **Start→Word** and open a new document.

2. Type the following paragraph.

    Do not press Enter *until the end of the paragraph. Let Word Wrap move your words to the next line for you. Your lines may end at different places than they do in this example.*

    ```
    It is important to sit correctly at a computer to keep
    yourself from pain. You should sit in a comfortable chair
    that supports your back. Your eyes should be almost as high
    as the top of the screen. Your forearms should be parallel
    to the floor. Keep your wrists straight. Your feet should
    be flat on the floor. Relax your shoulders. Enter
    ```

3. Choose **File→Print→Print** to print your work.

4. Close Word. Click **Don't Save** when Word asks if you wish to save your work.

· ·

▶ SKILL BUILDER 4.4 **Type a Paragraph**

In this exercise, you will type a paragraph. Then you will print the paragraph.

1. Open Word: **Start→Word** (or your version) and open a new document.

2. Type a paragraph about why you want to speak English well.

3. Choose **File→Print→Print** to print your work.

4. Close Word. Click **Don't Save** when Word asks if you wish to save your work.

· ·

# Paired Conversation

With a partner, take turns reading the A and B parts of the conversation.

Partner A	Hello. Are you learning to use the computer?
Partner B	Yes, I am.
Partner A	Will you show me how to type a résumé so I can look for a job?
Partner B	Yes. We will learn how to do that later. First, we need to learn to use the Word program.
Partner A	I do not know how to do that.
Partner B	To open Word, first click the Start button. Then click Word.
Partner A	Oh! I see "Word" on the title bar!
Partner B	Do you see the cursor blinking on the screen?
Partner A	Yes, I do.
Partner B	The computer is telling you that it is ready for you to type your text.
Partner A	Is there anything else I should know before I start?
Partner B	Yes. At the end of a paragraph, press the Enter key.
Partner A	Okay. Anything else?
Partner B	You can also erase a word with the Backspace key.
Partner A	Thanks so much for helping me.
Partner B	You're welcome.

Chapter Review

▶ 4.1 Fill in the Computer Keyboard

Exercise A

On each key in this picture of the keyboard, write the letter, number, or symbol from your computer keyboard. (Your keyboard may look a little different.)

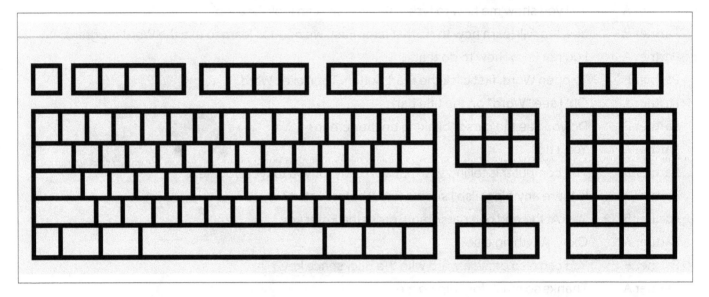

Exercise B

After you have finished labeling the keyboard, draw hands with the fingers on the correct keys for typing.

Identify and Match

Match the items in Column 1 with the correct text in Column 2. Write the correct letter from Column 2 on the line next to the number in Column 1.

COLUMN 1

_____ **1.** Shift key

_____ **2.** Word Wrap

_____ **3.** Delete key

_____ **4.** Word

_____ **5.** Backspace key

_____ **6.** Cursor

COLUMN 2

A. A blinking line that shows where the computer will put the next word

B. A powerful word processor that you must buy separately and install on a computer

C. The key that deletes letters to the left (←) of the cursor; you remove one letter or space each time you tap it

D. A key that helps make a capital letter or the top symbol of a typed key

E. The key that deletes letters to the right (→) of the cursor; you remove one letter or space each time you tap it

F. When you are typing and reach the end of a line, this feature will automatically put the next words you type on the next line for you

CHAPTER 5

More with Word

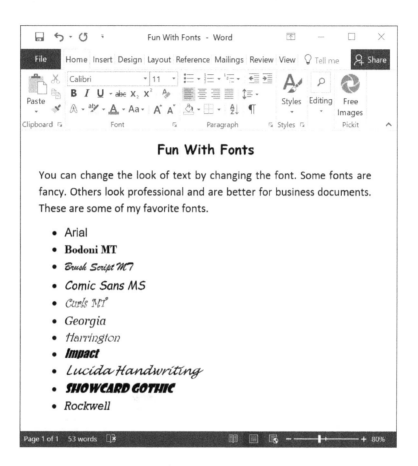

Computer Objectives

- Save and name a file

- Format and align text in various ways

- Add bullets to a list

- Use a USB drive

Language Objectives

- Use appropriate words to describe saving and naming files

- Describe how to format and align text

- Tell a partner how to perform tasks learned in this chapter

 # Vocabulary

Picture Dictionary – Nouns

A **noun** is the name of a person, place, or thing. The following nouns are introduced in this chapter:

1. **Document** – A typed record that provides information

2. **Alignment** – How text is placed, either on the left, center, or right side of the page

left   center   right

NOTE! The word *alignment* is a synonym for the words *placement* and *location*.

3. **USB (Universal Serial Bus) drive** – A small tool used to save computer files; you can use it in different computers

4. **USB port** – A small opening on the CPU where you insert a USB drive

5. **Font** – The shape and size of typed letters

FRIENDS:
Adam
Steven
Mario

6. **Bullets** – Special dots, squares, checkmarks, or characters that you can place before items on a list

7. **Bold type** – A style of lettering where the letters are thicker and darker

NOTE! A suffix is a part of a word that comes at the end of the word. Examples: *thick* and *thicker* (more thick); *dark* and *darker* (more dark).

8. **Italic type** – A style of lettering where the letters are a little slanted to the right

Computer Verbs

A **verb** tells an action or what a subject is or does. The following verbs are introduced in this chapter:

VERB	MEANING	EXAMPLE
1. **Save**	To keep your work on a document in the computer so you can use it again later	*I want to **save** this letter so I can remember what I wrote.*
2. **Insert**	To put a USB drive into the USB port of a computer	*I have a document on this USB drive. I will **insert** it in the USB port so I can open the document I need.*
3. **Increase**	To make bigger	*I can't read the words. I'm going to **increase** the font size so the words appear larger.*
4. **Decrease**	To make smaller	*The letters are too big and the document is on two pages. Please **decrease** the font size so the document fits on one page.*
5. **Align**	To place on the left, center, or right side of the page	*In most documents we type, we **align** the text on the left side of the page.*
6. **Scroll**	To move the contents of a window up, down, right, or left	*When you use the Font menu, you have to **scroll** down to find the font you like.*
7. **Highlight**	To click at the beginning of a letter and drag with the mouse to the end of what you want to change	*To change the text of this sentence, you have to **highlight** it first.*
8. **Format** (font)	To pick the font you want and use it in your document	*I don't like the font on this letter, so I am going to **format** it with a new font type.*
9. **Right-click**	To press and release the right mouse button	*You usually left-click the mouse button, but sometimes you have to **right-click** it.*

 Concepts and Exercises

Highlighting Text

To change the format of text, you must highlight it first. You can see that text is highlighted when the background becomes blue (or another color), as shown here.

A Text not highlighted   **B** Text highlighted

It is fun to change the format of my text. It makes my work look better. Formatting also makes my words more interesting and easy to read. I can show which words are important.

HOW TO HIGHLIGHT TEXT

Steps A–C show one way to highlight text, by dragging with the mouse.

NOTE! You can highlight text from the beginning to the end or from the end to the beginning.

A. Click to the left of the first word in the text you want to highlight.

B. Hold down the left mouse button and then move down and to the right as you continue to hold down the mouse button (dragging).

It is fun to change the format of my text. It makes my work look better.
Formatting also makes my words more interesting and easy to read. I can show
which words are important.

C. Let go of the mouse button when all of the text is selected.

HOW TO REMOVE THE HIGHLIGHTING

Click anywhere away from the highlighted words to take off the highlighting. You can also click once within the highlighted words to remove the highlighting.

▶ EXERCISE 5.1

In this exercise, you will type text in Word and then drag with the mouse to highlight some of the text.

1. Open Word: **Start→Word** and click **Blank Document**.

2. Type this paragraph in Word:

   ```
   It is fun to change the format of my text. It makes my
   work look better. Formatting also makes my words more
   interesting and easy to read. I can show which words are
   important.
   ```

   Now you will highlight the first sentence.

3. Move your cursor to the end of the first sentence.

   It is fun to change the format of my text. It makes my work look better.
   Formatting also makes my words more interesting and easy to read. I can show
   which words are important.

4. Hold down the mouse button and move to the left until the first sentence is highlighted.

   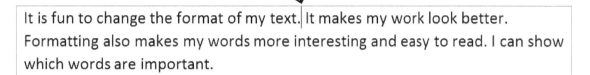

   It is fun to change the format of my text. It makes my work look better.
   Formatting also makes my words more interesting and easy to read. I can show
   which words are important.

   The highlighted text is also called a selection.

5. Let go of the mouse button.

6. Click on a clear part of the Word window (away from the highlight) to remove the highlight.

   Leave Word open. You will soon learn something new to do with a selection.

Formatting Text

Formatting makes the text that you type look better. One way you can make it look different is by changing the font shape and size. Here are some examples of different font types:

FONT NAME	EXAMPLE
Calibri	This text is formatted with the Calibri font.
Arial Black	**This text is formatted with the Arial Black font.**
French Script	*This text is formatted with the French Script font.*
Papyrus	This text is formatted with the Papyrus font.

NOTE! In this chapter, the word *format* is used in the present tense, as a gerund, and in the past tense. For example, notice the spelling change in the words *format*, *formatting*, and *formatted*.

Fonts can be different sizes.

10 pt.	12 pt.	18 pt.	24 pt.	36 pt.
ABC	ABC	ABC	ABC	ABC

Here are some other ways to format text:

Normal	Bold	Italics	Underline
ABC	**ABC**	*ABC*	<u>ABC</u>

To change the format of any text, you must highlight it first.

The Word Ribbon

One way to format text you have highlighted is to use the Ribbon. (If you do not see the icons on your Ribbon, click the Home tab.) Some features of the Word Ribbon are shown here:

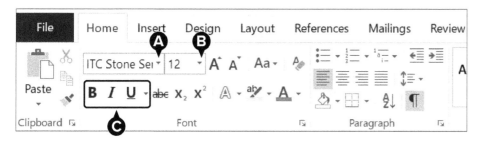

Ⓐ You can use the Font drop-down list arrow to change the font type.

Ⓑ You can use Font Size drop-down list arrow to change the font size.

Ⓒ Use these buttons to add bold, italic, or underline. Watch your text change as you change the font settings.

NOTE! You must highlight the text before you can make these changes using the Ribbon tools.

▶ EXERCISE 5.2

In this exercise, you will highlight text and apply a font format to it.

1. Highlight the word **fun** in the first sentence, as in the picture.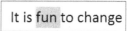

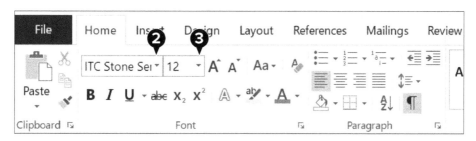

2. Click the **Font** drop-down arrow and then click **Arial Black**. (You may have to scroll up or down to see it.)

3. Click the **Font Size** drop-down arrow and then click **16**.

4. Highlight the word **work** in the second sentence on the first line so you can change the font type and format of that word.

5. Click the **Bold** B button.

6. Click the **Font** drop-down arrow and then click **Courier New**. (You may need to scroll down to find it.)

7. Click the **Italic** $\boxed{I}$ button.

8. Click the **Font Size** drop-down arrow and then click **16**.

See how the word work *looks different now. Leave Word open.*

Bullets

You add bullets to make lines of text look more like a list. Bullets can look like squares, dots, checkmarks, or other characters.

Days of the Week	Days of the Week
Sunday	• Sunday
Monday	• Monday
Tuesday	• Tuesday
Wednesday	• Wednesday
Thursday	• Thursday
Friday	• Friday
Saturday	• Saturday

Lists of the days of the week without and with bullets

HOW TO ADD BULLETS

A. Highlight the lines where you want the bullets.

B. Click the Bullets $\boxed{\vdots\equiv}$ button on the Home tab of the Ribbon.

Days of the Week
Sunday
Monday
Tuesday
Wednesday
Thursday
Friday
Saturday

▶ EXERCISE 5.3

In this exercise, you will type a new list and add bullets to it.

1. Click with your mouse at the very end of the last line of text.

2. Press ⌈Enter⌋.

Now your screen should look like this.

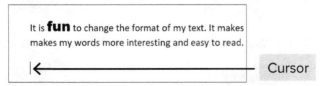

It is **fun** to change the format of my text. It makes makes my words more interesting and easy to read.

← Cursor

3. Type **These are some of my formatting tools:** and then press ⏎`Enter`
   two times.

4. Type this list of formatting tools. Press ⏎`Enter` after each line, as shown.

   Alignment⏎`Enter`
   Font type⏎`Enter`
   Font size⏎`Enter`
   Bold⏎`Enter`
   Italic⏎`Enter`
   Bullets⏎`Enter`

5. Highlight all of the formatting tools.

6. Click the **Bullets** ⊞ button in the Paragraph group on the Ribbon.

7. Click anywhere on a clear part of the screen to make the highlight disappear.

   Now the list should look like this:

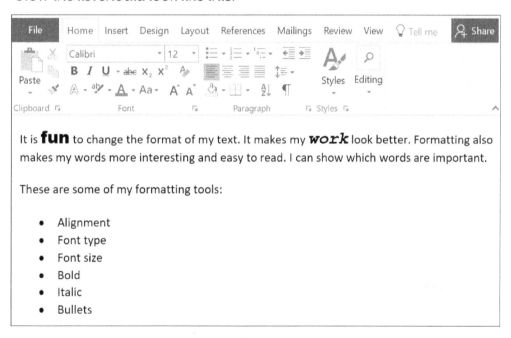

   Leave Word open.

Alignment

You can use the buttons on the Home tab of the Word Ribbon to change the alignment of a line. Word lets you choose three kinds of alignment.

Left ☰	Center ☰	Right ☰
This is aligned left.	This is aligned center.	This is aligned right.

HOW TO CHANGE THE ALIGNMENT

A. Click anywhere in the line or paragraph you want to change.

B. Click the button for the kind of alignment you want.

▶ EXERCISE 5.4

In this exercise, you will create a title for your document and change its alignment to Center.

1. Use the mouse or arrow keys to go to the very top of your document.

2. Press [Enter] two times.

3. Use the **up arrow** [↑] key to go back to the top of the document.

4. Type **Formatting Text** as the title.

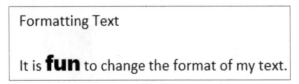

Formatting Text

It is **fun** to change the format of my text.

5. Click the **Center** alignment button on the Ribbon.

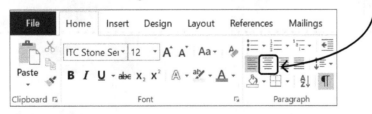

Word moves the title to the center of the screen. Leave Word open.

Saving Your Work

In the following exercises, you will save your work to a USB drive. When you save your work on a USB drive, you can move it to different computers. You can also open work you did earlier and add to it or change it.

To save work to a USB drive, you must first insert the USB drive into the USB port on a CPU or laptop.

HOW TO INSERT A USB DRIVE INTO A USB PORT

A. Find the USB port on the CPU. It can be on the front, side, or back of the computer.

B. Gently push the USB drive into the USB port.

- If it does not go into the port, turn it over and try again.
- You should be able to easily push it all the way in.

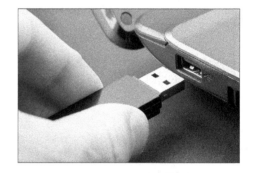

C. If any windows automatically open on the desktop, close them.

Computer Files

When you save your work on the computer, it is saved in a package called a file. Each file must be given a name so you can find it again when you need it. Once you save work to a file, you can open it again later with the same program. The process of storing a file is called *saving*.

- Central Valley
- Chapter 5
- Cities
- computers
- Emergency
- Famous Americans
- Fun With Fonts

Examples of computer files

HOW TO SAVE A FILE

A. Create some work in a computer program. For example, type a document in Word.

B. Choose File→Save As→Browse.

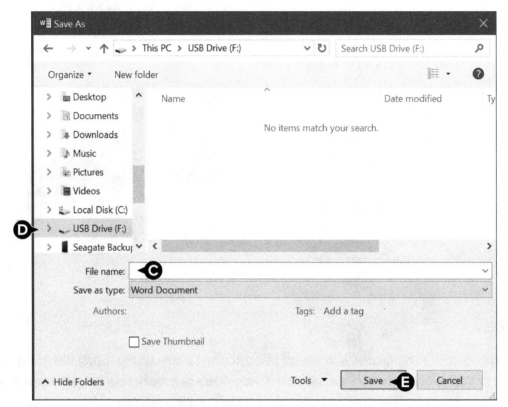

C. Type the filename. You do not have to click in this space because the cursor is already there.

D. Click your USB drive (usually E: or F:) in the Navigation pane on the left side of the dialog box. You may have to scroll down to see it. USB drives can have different icons and names.

E. Click the Save button.

After you finish your computer work, you must remove (take out) the USB drive properly.

HOW TO SAFELY REMOVE A USB DRIVE

A. Click the Safely Remove Hardware and Eject Media button on the taskbar at the bottom-right side of the screen.

If you do not see it, you may have to click Show Hidden Icons ^ *to make it show.*

B. From the pop-up menu, choose Eject USB Flash Memory. Your USB drive may show a different name after *Eject.*

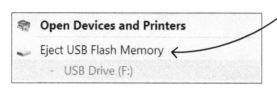

C. Now it is safe to pull your USB drive out of the USB port.

▶ EXERCISE 5.5

In this exercise, you will save the work that is in Word now. Your USB drive should be inserted into the computer. If any new windows open, close them.

1. Choose **File→Save As→Browse**.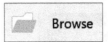

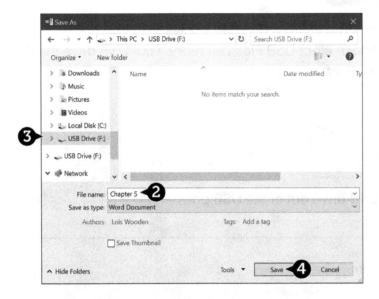

2. Type **Chapter 5** in the File Name box.

3. In the Navigation pane, click the icon for your USB drive. If you do not see it, scroll down to find it.

4. Click **Save**.

   Word saves your work to the USB drive.

5. Close Word.

. . . .

⬤ Skill Builder Exercises

▶ **SKILL BUILDER 5.1 Change the Font**

In this exercise, you will change fonts in a Word document.

1. Open Word: **Start→Word** and open a blank document.

2. Type this paragraph.

    Do not press Enter *until the very end.*

    Eating healthy foods will make us look and feel better. I know eating right will help us not to get sick. I will use my computer to make a grocery list so I remember to buy healthy foods. After I finish the list, I will print it so I can take it to the grocery store. When I get back home, I will make a special lunch for you. You will be surprised at how good it tastes!

3. Highlight the first sentence.

4. Change the font to **Lucida Bright**. Change the size to **14** and then click the **Bold** button.

5. Click just to the left of the "I" at the beginning of the second sentence and press Enter.

6. Click in the middle of the first sentence and then click the **Center** ☰ alignment button.

    When you are finished, your screen should look like this.

> ### Eating healthy foods will make us look and feel better.
>
> I know eating right will help us not to get sick. I will use my computer to make a grocery list so I remember to buy healthy foods. After I finish the list, I will print it so I can take it to the grocery store. When I get back home, I will make a special lunch for you. You will be surprised at how good it tastes!

7. Save the file as: **Healthy Foods** (save it to your USB drive)

8. Choose **File→Print→Print** to print your work.

9. Close Word.

▶ SKILL BUILDER 5.2 **Type a Bulleted List**

In this exercise, you will type a list with bullets.

1. Open Word: **Start→Word** and open a blank document.

2. Type these words, pressing Enter where shown:

   United States Holidays Enter
   New Year's Day Enter
   Martin Luther King Day Enter
   Presidents' Day Enter
   Easter Enter
   Memorial Day Enter
   Fourth of July Enter
   Labor Day Enter
   Thanksgiving Enter
   Christmas Enter

3. Highlight the first line.

4. Change the font to **Bold** and any size and style that you like.

5. Highlight all lines of words except the top one.

6. Click the **Bullets** button on the Ribbon.

7. Save the file as **Holidays** to your USB drive.

8. Print your work and then close Word.

....

▶ SKILL BUILDER 5.3 **Change the Alignment**

In this exercise, you will change the text alignment.

1. Open Word: **Start→Word** and open a blank document.

2. Read these notes and then type the text you see on the next page.

   ■ Press Enter where shown.

   ■ Do not type the blank lines at the ends of the sentences.

   ■ Type your own name on the first line where it says *Name*.

   ■ At the end of line 3, type the name of the city where you were born.

   ■ At the end of line 4, type the year you came to the United States. If you were born here, type the year you were born.

   ■ At the end of line 5, type the name of the city where you live now.

This is the text to type:

Name Enter Enter

My History Enter Enter

I was born in _____ . Enter

I arrived in the United States in _____ . Enter

Now I live in _____ . Enter

3. Highlight the first line and then click **Align Right** ☰.

4. Highlight the second line and then click the **Center** ☰ button to center it.

5. Click in one of the last three lines. They are already aligned to the left, so you will see **Align Left** selected on the Ribbon.

Here is an example of how your screen should look.

                                           Narghes Aria

My History

I was born in Tehran.
I arrived in the United States in 2019.
Now I live in Boston.

6. Save the file as **My History** to your USB drive.

7. Print your work and then close Word.

▶ SKILL BUILDER 5.4 **Create a List**

In this exercise, you will create your own bulleted list.

1. Open Word: **Start→Word** and open a blank document.

2. Type the title: **My Favorite Cities in the World**

3. Click the **Center** ≡ button to align the title in the center of the page.

4. Press Enter two times and then click **Align Left** ≣ to move the cursor to the left side of the screen.

5. Type a list of ten cities in the world. Press Enter after the name of each city.

6. Give each city a different font type.

7. Highlight all of the cities.

7. Click the **Bullets** ⠵☰ button.

8. Save the file as **Cities** to your USB drive.

9. Print your work and then close Word.

Paired Conversation

With a partner, take turns reading the A and B parts of the conversation.

NOTE! This conversation uses the future tense, as seen in *going* to and *will*. When you use helping verbs like these, you also need a main verb.

This conversation also uses contractions. When you put two words together, an apostrophe shows that a letter (or letters) has been left out. Here are the contractions used in this conversation:

Full Words	Contraction
We will	We'll
That is	That's
Do not	Don't
I will	I'll
I am	I'm

Partner A	Today's lesson is going to be fun.
Partner B	Really? Why?
Partner A	We are going to learn how to format our text.
Partner B	I heard someone say that we will learn about fonts.
Partner A	Yes, we will learn how to change our text.
Partner B	That sounds like fun!
Partner A	I know. We'll also learn how to make bold text.
Partner B	That's good, but I like the way italic text looks better.
Partner A	Well, we will learn both!
Partner B	Did you bring your USB drive?
Partner A	Yes, I did, but I don't know how to insert it in the computer.
Partner B	I'll show you how to put it in the USB port.
Partner A	Thanks. I don't want to mess it up.
Partner B	We can put all this new formatting in our own documents.
Partner A	Do you think we will be able to print today?
Partner B	I think so.
Partner A	We have a nice printer in the classroom.
Partner B	Well, I'm going to be the first one to print my document!

Chapter Review

5.1 Fill in the Blanks

Write the correct word (or words) in each blank for the following sentences about USB drives.

WORD BANK			
bottom	Eject	turn	taskbar
insert	USB port	easily	safe

Inserting and Removing a USB Drive

1. Find the _____ _____ on the CPU. It can be on the front or back of the computer.

2. Gently _____ the USB drive into the USB port. If it does not go into the port _____, _____ it over and try it again.

Taking Out a USB Drive Safely

3. Click the Safely Remove Hardware and Eject Media button on the _____ at the _____-right side of the screen. If you do not see it, you may have to click the Show Hidden Icons button to make it show.

4. From the pop-up menu, click _____ USB Flash Memory.

5. Now it is _____ to pull your USB drive out of the USB port.

5.2 Verb Worksheet

Fill in the blanks. Select the best answer for each sentence using the computer verbs in the Word Bank.

WORD BANK		
save	decrease	highlight
insert	align	format
increase	scroll	right-click

1. To bring text into line on the left or right side or in the center is to

   _____ text.

2. To _____ means to keep what you did on a document in the

   computer so you can use it again later.

3. To pick the font you want and use it in your document is to _____.

4. To _____ means to put a USB drive into the USB port of a computer.

5. To make your text smaller in size is to _____ it.

6. To _____ text, you click at the beginning of a letter and drag the

   mouse to the end of what you want to change.

7. To press and release the right mouse button is to _____.

8. To _____ means to move the contents of a window up, down, right,

   or left.

9. To _____ the text means to make the text bigger in size.

CHAPTER 6

The Internet

Computer Objectives

- Open and use Google Chrome
- Use a search engine to find information
- Type an Internet address to go to a website
- Apply for a job online

Language Objectives

- Use vocabulary words to describe opening and using Google Chrome
- Describe actions to take when using a search engine
- Use appropriate verbs when describing how to find information on the Internet
- Talk about typing addresses in the address bar
- Tell a partner how to go to a website

Learning Resources: **boostyourskills.lablearning.com**

 Vocabulary

Picture Dictionary – Nouns

A **noun** is the name of a person, place, or thing. The following nouns are introduced in this chapter:

1. **Internet** – Computers from all over the world connected so they can communicate

2. **Modem** – A tool that connects your computer to the Internet

3. **Link** – An object or text that takes you from one web page to another when you click it

4. **Internet connection** – The system that lets you contact the Internet

5. **Website** – A place on the Internet where you can find information by using a search engine or an Internet address

6. **Internet address** – The unique address for each web page

7. **Web browser** – Software that lets you connect to the Internet

8. **Simulation** – An exercise that is not real; it is planned ahead of time, with all the possibilities already set

9. **ISP (Internet service provider)** – A company that gives you a connection to the Internet; usually, you pay money for this service

10. **Homepage** – The web page that appears when you open Google Chrome or another web browser

11. **Search engine** – A website you can use to look for things on the Internet

12. **ScreenTip** – A small message that comes up when you hold your mouse pointer on top of it

Computer Verbs

A **verb** tells an action or what a subject is or does. The following verbs are introduced in this chapter:

VERB	MEANING	EXAMPLE
1. **Browse**	To look around on the Internet	*I need some ideas for a gift, so I'm going to **browse** the Internet to see what I can find.*
2. **Connect**	To make contact with the Internet	*I will **connect** to the Internet to find the information I need.*
3. **Search**	To look for information on a specific topic on the Internet	*I am writing a book report. I will **search** the Internet for facts about my topic.*
4. **Visit**	To look at a website	*I have a few minutes to **visit** my favorite news website.*

Concepts and Exercises

What Is the Internet?

The Internet is millions of computers from all parts of the world connected so they can communicate. To join the Internet, you must have an Internet connection, which you get by signing up with an Internet service provider (ISP). For most types of connections, you need a modem.

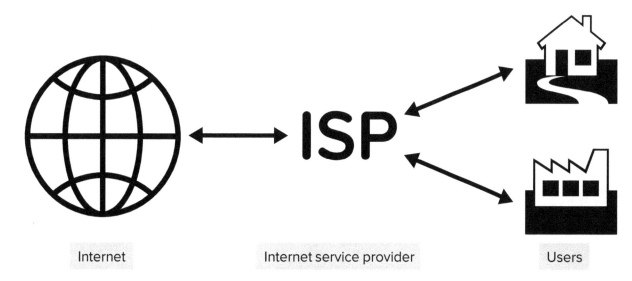

| Internet | Internet service provider | Users |

Types of Internet Connections

There are different ways to connect to the Internet. They have different speeds and costs. For each type of connection, you should be able to find a few different ISPs in your area.

- **Dial-up** – This uses a regular telephone line to connect to the Internet. Dial-up costs less money than other types of connections. It is the slowest type of connection.

- **Cable** – This connection uses the same cable as cable television.

- **DSL** – You must have a special telephone line to use this type of connection.

- **Satellite** – A cable connects you to a satellite dish, which communicates with a satellite for Internet access.

- **Wi-Fi** – Wireless networking sends the Internet data through the air. No wires or cables are needed.

Google Chrome

You need special software on your computer to connect to the Internet. This software is called an Internet (or web) browser. Many people use Google Chrome as their browser. Other popular browsers are Microsoft Edge and Mozilla Firefox. You can read more about those browsers on the Internet. In this book, we will use Google Chrome.

NOTE! Most people just call it Chrome.

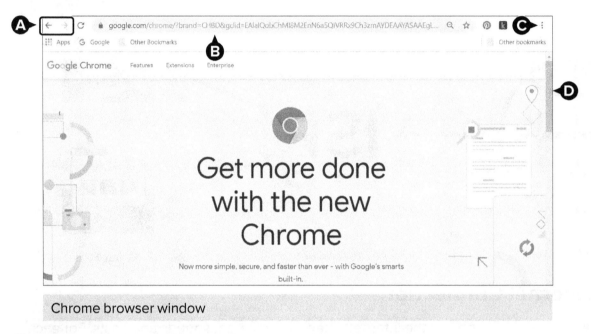

Chrome browser window

A **Back and Forward buttons** – These buttons help you move among websites.

B **Address bar** – In this bar, you can see the Internet address of the website you are visiting. You can also click in it and type the address of a website you want to visit.

C **Chrome menu button** – Chrome has a special menu for using the Internet. You can open it by clicking the Chrome menu button.

D **Scroll bar** – This bar lets you move to other parts of the web page that you can't see on the screen.

▶ EXERCISE 6.1

In this exercise, you will start Chrome.

1. Click the **Google Chrome** button on the taskbar.

If you don't see the button, choose Start→Google Chrome. (You may have to scroll to the "G" section.)

The Google homepage opens. A homepage *is the first page a web browser shows when it is opened.*

2. Point with your mouse (don't click) on the Back button. Watch for the ScreenTip to come up.

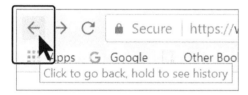

3. Put your mouse over other icons. Watch for the ScreenTips to show on each one.

Leave the Chrome window open.

The Address Bar

When you click in the address bar once, the address there becomes highlighted. Then you can type in a new address. You do not have to use [Backspace] or [Delete] if the address is highlighted.

▶ EXERCISE 6.2

In this exercise, you will type an address in the address bar. Chrome should still be open.

1. Click in the white part of the **address bar** and see that the address is highlighted.

🔒 Secure | https://www.google.com

Google   Other Bookmarks

2. Type **www.yahoo.com** and press Enter to go to the new website.

🔒 Secure | https://www.yahoo.com

3. Take a minute to look at this website.

4. Click the **Back** ← button to go back to the homepage.

Remember, the place where you start when you open Chrome is called the homepage.

. . . .

Search Engines

A search engine is a website made to look for things on the Internet. Google is one of the many search engines you can use. Other popular search engines are Yahoo and Bing. They look different, but they usually have search tools like the ones in Google.

Ⓐ The name of the search engine appears in the middle of the web page.

Ⓑ Links can be words or pictures. When you click a link, you go to another web page. When you place your mouse pointer over a link, the mouse pointer changes to a hand symbol 👆.

Ⓒ You type what you are looking for in the Search box.

Ⓓ You press Enter to start the search.

▶ EXERCISE 6.3

In this exercise, you will use a simulation of a search engine to practice finding information. Using a simulation ensures the process will remain constant even if the real web page changes.

1. Start Chrome by clicking the button on the taskbar or by choosing **Start→Google Chrome**, if it is not already open.

2. Click once in the **address bar**. Type `boostyourskills.lablearning.com` and tap `Enter`.

3. Click the **View Resources** button under the picture of your book and then click the **Chapter Resources** tab.

4. Click **Chapter 6: The Internet** to see that section and then click **Exercise 6.3**.

5. Click **Start** to begin the simulation.

   You will complete the rest of the exercise in the simulation.

6. Click the **Close** button.

Search Results

When the search engine gives you the results, take a few minutes to look at them and decide which ones have what you are searching for. Sometimes you have to look at a few to find what you want. You can add other words to your search if you cannot find what you are searching for.

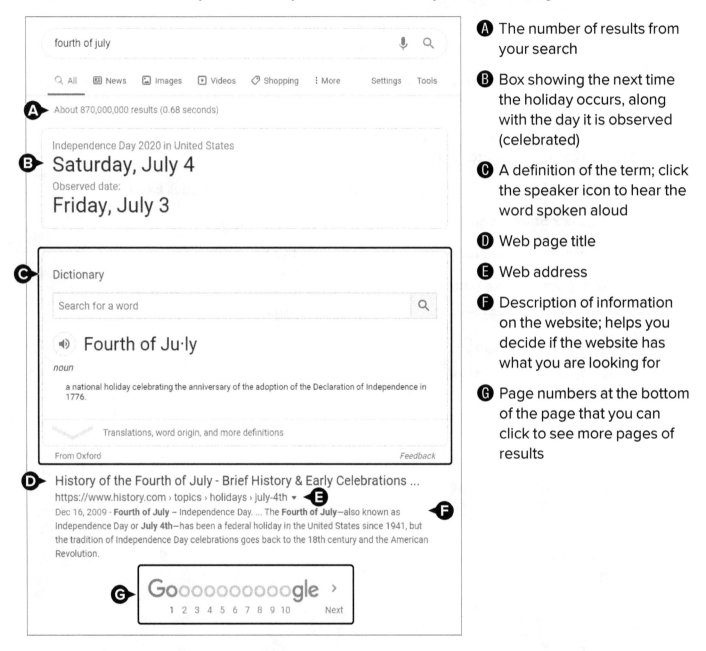

A The number of results from your search

B Box showing the next time the holiday occurs, along with the day it is observed (celebrated)

C A definition of the term; click the speaker icon to hear the word spoken aloud

D Web page title

E Web address

F Description of information on the website; helps you decide if the website has what you are looking for

G Page numbers at the bottom of the page that you can click to see more pages of results

NOTE! These results are only from one search engine. They change every day and look different on different computers in different places.

More About Scroll Bars

You use scroll bars to move around in a window. They let you go to parts of the web page that do not show because they are too long or too wide to fit on the screen. The scroll bars let you move around to see the rest of the web page.

You cannot see the whole web page without scrolling.

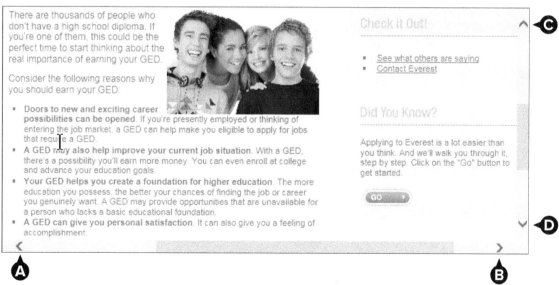

A Horizontal scroll bar

B Vertical scroll bar

After using the vertical and horizonal scroll bars, you can read the web page.

A Click the left arrow of the horizontal scroll bar to move to the left.

B Click the right arrow of the horizontal scroll bar to move to the right.

C Click the top arrow of the vertical scroll bar to go up.

D Click the bottom arrow of the vertical scroll bar to go down.

▶ EXERCISE 6.4

In this exercise, you will use a simulation of a search engine to practice finding information.

1. If necessary, type **boostyourskills.lablearning.com** into the address bar of your web browser and tap ⌷Enter⌷.

2. Click the **View Resources** button under the picture of your book and then click the **Chapter Resources** tab.

3. Click **Chapter 6: The Internet** to see that section and then click **Exercise 6.4**.

4. Click **Start** to begin the simulation.

   You will complete the rest of the exercise in the simulation.

5. Click the **Close** button.

6. Close Chrome.

. . . .

Search for a Job Online

Many jobs can only be found on the Internet. Searching for a job online takes some practice and time, but it is easier than visiting businesses one by one. These days, most people find their jobs online. Once you find the job that you want, you can apply to it from the Internet. It is easy to communicate with companies that interest you by email. You will learn to email in Chapter 7, "Email."

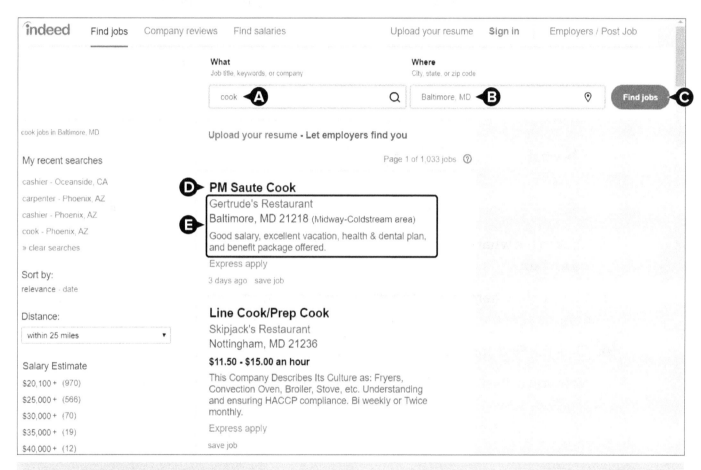

An example of a job search website

A The place where you type the kind of job you want to search for

B The place where you enter the city and state where you want to work

C Search button

D Job title

E Information about the job

▶ EXERCISE 6.5

In this exercise, you will use Indeed.com, a job search website, to practice looking for a job. There are many job search websites. You can use Google or another search engine to look for more. Most of the others work the same way as Indeed.

NOTE! Remember that sometimes websites change, but they usually still work the same or similarly.

1. Open Chrome. Click in the **address bar** and then type `indeed.com` and press `Enter`.

2. Click in the **what** box and type the kind of job you want to find; for example: `cashier`

3. Click in the **where** box and type the city and state where you want to work. Type a comma after the name of the city, before the name of the state.

4. Click the **Find Jobs** button.

   Now you will see a list of jobs close to the place where you want to work.

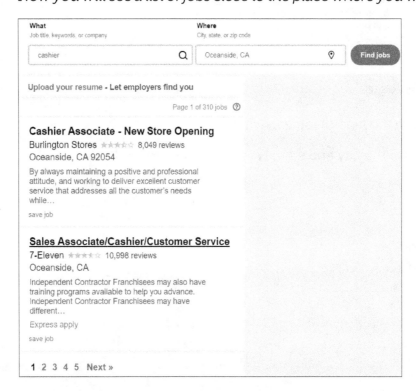

5. Scroll down the list using the scroll bar on the right side. At the bottom of the web page, you will see numbers you can click to go to more pages with jobs.

6. Click the name of a job so you can read about it. Usually there is a link to apply for the job.

7. When you are finished looking at one job, click the **Close** ⊠ button at the top of the web page to close that browser tab. You should now be back to the job list so you can look at other jobs.

8. When you have finished looking at the list of jobs, search for a different job by typing in the **what** and **where** boxes at the top of the web page.

9. When you are finished searching for jobs, close Chrome.

· ·

Apply for a Job Online

Once you have searched the Internet and found a job that you would like, you can apply for it online. You will need all of your employment information and a résumé. You will create your résumé in Chapter 10, "Editing Word Documents."

▶ EXERCISE 6.6

 In this exercise, you will use a simulation to see what it is like to fill out a job application form on the Internet.

1. Open Chrome, type **boostyourskills.lablearning.com** into the address bar and tap ⎡Enter⎤, and then click the **View Resources** button for your book title.

2. Click the the **Chapter Resources** tab, click **Chapter 6: The Internet** to see that section, and then click **Exercise 6.6**.

3. Click **Start** to begin the simulation.

   You will complete the rest of the exercise in the simulation.

4. Close Chrome.

· ·

Skill Builder Exercises

▶ SKILL BUILDER 6.1 **Go to Another Website**

In this exercise, you will go to a website using the address bar.

1. Click the **Google Chrome** button on the taskbar (or choose **Start→Google Chrome**).

2. Click once in the **address bar**. Then, type `accuweather.com` and press Enter.

3. Look for the search box near the top of the page.

   It may look a little different because websites change.

4. Click in the **search box**, type the name of a city, and then click the **Search** button.

   Don't worry if there is another name there; just click and type.

5. After you click the **Search** button, you will see a list of cities. Click the name of the city that you are looking for.

6. Read the weather forecast. Use the scroll bar arrow on the right to scroll down.

7. Move your mouse around. You will see the hand show when you are on a link.

8. Click any of the links that look interesting to you.

   Watch for the mouse pointer to change to the hand before you click.

9. Click the **Back** ← button until you return to the homepage.

▶ SKILL BUILDER 6.2 **Search the Internet**

In this exercise, you will search using Google.com.

1. Click in the **address bar**; type **www.google.com** and press Enter.

2. Click in the **search box**; type **US citizenship test questions** and press Enter.

3. Look at the results that come up. Read the descriptions carefully.

4. Scroll down to see more search results.

5. Pick out one site you think has the information you are looking for and click its web page title.

6. When the web page opens, look to see if it shows what you want.

7. When you finish reading, click the **Back** ← button.

8. Try one of the other results by clicking its title.

9. When you find a web page that shows some of the citizenship questions, read them.

10. Close Chrome.

▶ SKILL BUILDER 6.3 Search for a State Governor

In this exercise, you will use the Google.com search engine to find information about someone in your state.

1. Use Google.com to search for information about the governor of the state where you live.

2. Click some of the web page titles to see what information appears.

3. To print one of the pages about the governor, first click the **menu** ⋮ button on the Chrome toolbar.

4. Click **Print** and then click **Print** again.

Paired Conversation

With a partner, take turns reading the A and B parts of the conversation.

Partner A	I'm a new student.
Partner B	Welcome to our classroom!
Partner A	I heard that today's class is about the Internet.
Partner B	That's right.
Partner A	Which websites will we visit?
Partner B	I'm not sure. We'll have to use a search engine.
Partner A	Is that what you use to look for things on the Internet?
Partner B	That's right.
Partner A	Well, let's visit an interesting website.
Partner B	I know! Let's go to our school's homepage first.
Partner A	That's a great idea. Let's connect to it now.
Partner B	Well, let's type the Internet address for our school in the address bar.
Partner A	Okay. Now what do I do?
Partner B	We can use the links to go to the pages we want.
Partner A	Thanks. Now I want to browse the Internet.
Partner B	You'll have to wait. We have to do a simulation exercise first.
Partner A	Okay.
Partner B	Later, we can search for other interesting subjects.

Chapter Review

6.1   Fill in the Blanks

Write the correct words to describe the parts of the Chrome window.

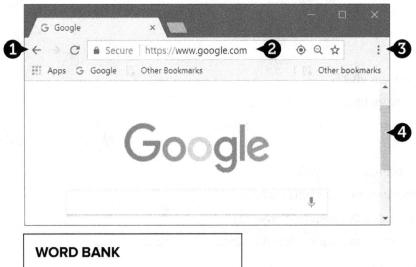

WORD BANK

address bar	Back button
menu button	scroll bar

1. The _____ helps you move to websites that you have just visited.

2. In the _____, you can see the Internet address of the website you are visiting. You can also click here and type the address of the website you want to go to.

3. The Chrome _____ opens a special menu for using the Internet.

4. The _____ lets you move to other parts of the web page.

6.2 Paired Conversation and Language Practice

Fill in the blanks in the conversation below using the words in the Word Bank. Then, circle all prepositions used in the conversation. Finally, with a partner, take turns reading the A and B parts of the conversation.

TIP! Prepositions show the relationship between a noun or pronoun to another element in the sentence.

WORD BANK				
student	Internet	Internet address	websites	search engine
Internet	visit	go	homepage	connect
classroom	links	browse	simulation	search

Partner A   I'm a new _____.

Partner B   Welcome to our _____!

Partner A   I heard that today's class is about the _____.

Partner B   That's right.

Partner A   Which _____ will we visit?

Partner B   I'm not sure. We'll have to use a _____ _____.

Partner A   Is that what you use to look for things on the _____?

Partner B   That's right.

Partner A   Well, let's _____ an interesting website.

Partner B   I know! Let's _____ to our school's _____ first.

Partner A   That's a great idea. Let's _____ to it now.

Partner B   Well, let's type the _____ _____ for our school in the address bar.

Partner A   Okay. Now what do I do?

Partner B   We can use the _____ to go to the pages we want.

Partner A   Thanks. Now I want to _____ the Internet.

Partner B   You'll have to wait. We have to do a _____ exercise first.

Partner A   Okay.

Partner B   Later, we can _____ for other interesting subjects.

CHAPTER 7

Email

Computer Objectives

- Sign in to email and send a message

- Reply to an email message

- Forward a message

Language Objectives

- Use vocabulary words to describe signing in to email

- Use computer verbs to describe actions taken with email messages

- Describe how to reply to and forward a message

Learning Resources: **boostyourskills.lablearning.com**

 # Vocabulary

Picture Dictionary – Nouns

A **noun** is the name of a person, place, or thing. The following nouns are introduced in this chapter:

1. **Message** – Information you type and send to another person using email

> Hello,
>
> This is my first email message.

2. **Button** – A small rectangle that completes an action when you click it

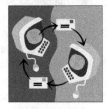

3. **Email (Electronic mail)** – A way to send information from one computer to another

4. **Password** – A personal word or combination of letters and numbers that lets you get into your email

`33366me`
`mary33now`

5. **Inbox** – A page in your email that lists all the messages you have received

6. **Username** – The name you choose for your personal email account

7. **Webmail** – An email service that allows you to reach your email account from your own computer, another computer, or a device such as a smartphone or tablet

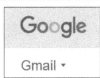

8. **"At" symbol** – The character included in email addresses between the username and the email service provider name

Computer Verbs

A **verb** tells an action or what a subject is or does. The following verbs are introduced in this chapter:

VERB	MEANING	EXAMPLE
1. **Compose**	To write a message	*I'll **compose** a message explaining my question and send it to my mentor.*
2. **Send**	To transmit a message from your email to another person's email	*I will **send** a message to my mother tomorrow.*
3. **Forward**	To send a message that you received to another person	*I received a wonderful message from Mary. I am going to **forward** it to Juan, so he can read it, too.*
4. **Reply**	To answer a message that you received	*My friend sent me a message saying that she is sick. I need to **reply** and ask her if she needs anything.*

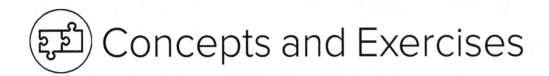 Concepts and Exercises

About Email

Email is a fast and easy way to communicate with people in all places in the world that have the Internet. You must have an email address and Internet access to use email.

- An email address must have three parts. It cannot have any spaces.

  Sample email address: student@gmail.com

USERNAME	AT SYMBOL	EMAIL SERVICE PROVIDER
student	@	gmail.com

- You will use webmail in this book. Webmail is useful because you can use it from any computer or device in the world that has Internet access.

- Many companies on the Internet offer free webmail. You can use a search engine to find the companies that do. Gmail is a popular webmail service. Some of the other free webmail companies are Outlook Mail, Yahoo, and Mail.com. You can use Google search to find other free webmail sites.

- All Internet service providers give you an email address when you sign up.

Getting an Email Account

When you get an email account, you must pick a username and a password.

- The username is any name that you use to access your email.

- The password must be entered to keep your email safe. No one can read your email unless they have your username and your password.

After you get an email account, you can send and receive email.

We will use Gmail as a webmail example. Different email programs look different, but most have the same parts and work the same or similarly. When you learn how to use Gmail, you will be able to use other email programs.

In this exercise, you will use a simulation to practice email before you try the real thing.

1. Click the **Google Chrome** 🔵 button on the taskbar at the bottom of your screen.

2. Click once in the **address bar**. Type **boostyourskills.lablearning.com** and tap ⌐Enter⌐.

3. Click the **View Resources** button under the picture of your book and then click the **Chapter Resources** tab.

4. Click **Chapter 7: Email** to see that section and then click **Exercise 7.1**.

5. Click **Start** to begin the simulation.

   You will complete the rest of the exercise in the simulation.

6. Click the **Close** button.

Writing and Sending a Message

Sending an email message is like writing a letter. You must add the email address of the person who will get the letter. Once you send an email, you cannot stop it. It will go where you sent it.

After you sign in to webmail, a window like this will show.

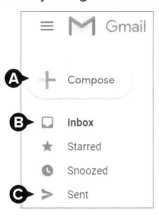
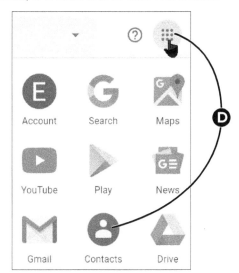

Ⓐ **Compose** – You click here to type a new message.

Ⓑ **Inbox** – This holds the email sent to you. You can click it to open it.

Ⓒ **Sent** – This holds email you have already sent. Click it to open it.

Ⓓ **Contacts** – You can click the Google apps button and choose Contacts to go to your contacts list. This is where you enter and keep people's email addresses.

▶ EXERCISE 7.2

 In this exercise, you will create (compose) and send a new email message.

1. If necessary, type **boostyourskills.lablearning.com** into the address bar of your web browser and tap [Enter]. Then, click the **View Resources** button under the picture of your book.

2. Click the **Chapter Resources** tab, click **Chapter 7: Email** to see that section, and then click **Exercise 7.2**.

3. Click **Start** to begin the simulation.

   You will complete the rest of the exercise in the simulation.

4. Click the **Close** button.

....

Contacts

Contacts is an address book in Gmail that holds a list of names and email addresses. Gmail lets you save names and email addresses in your Contacts address book to use again later.

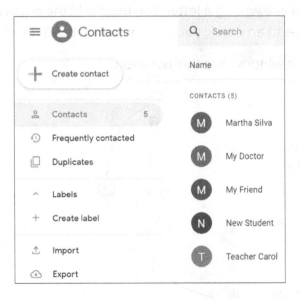

▶ EXERCISE 7.3

 In this exercise, you will add someone to your Contacts list.

1. If necessary, type **boostyourskills.lablearning.com** into the address bar of your web browser and tap [Enter]. Then, click the **View Resources** button under the picture of your book.

2. Click the **Chapter Resources** tab, click **Chapter 7: Email** to see that section, and then click **Exercise 7.3**.

3. Click **Start** to begin the simulation.

   You will complete the rest of the exercise in the simulation.

4. Click the **Close** button.

Reading Your Email

Once you receive an email, you will see it in your Inbox. Look at the information it shows.

| ☐ | Andy from Google | English, welcome to your new Google A | Dec 27 |

Ⓐ Name of the sender

Ⓑ Subject of the email

Ⓒ Date the email was sent (or the time if it was sent today)

You can read the email by clicking on the subject line.

▶ EXERCISE 7.4

In this exercise, you will check your mail, open a message, and print a message.

1. If necessary, type **boostyourskills.lablearning.com** into the address bar of your web browser and tap ⌨Enter. Then, click the **View Resources** button under the picture of your book.

2. Click the **Chapter Resources** tab, click **Chapter 7: Email** to see that section, and then click **Exercise 7.4**.

3. Click **Start** to begin the simulation.

   You will complete the rest of the exercise in the simulation.

4. Click the **Close** button.

Replying to Messages

When you want to answer a message, you reply to it. After you click the Reply button, Gmail takes you to a new window so you can type an answer to the email you received.

You will then see your cursor blinking at the top of the message box.

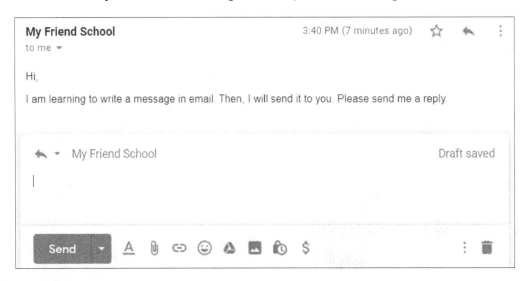

Ⓐ You can see the original message above the reply.

Ⓑ You can type your reply in the lower message box.

▶ EXERCISE 7.5

 In this exercise, you will send a reply to the email message you just opened.

1. If necessary, type **boostyourskills.lablearning.com** into the address bar of your web browser and tap Enter. Then, click the **View Resources** button under the picture of your book.

2. Click the **Chapter Resources** tab, click **Chapter 7: Email** to see that section, and then click **Exercise 7.5**.

3. Click **Start** to begin the simulation.

   You will complete the rest of the exercise in the simulation.

4. Click the **Close** button.

5. Close Chrome.

Skill Builder Exercises

▶ SKILL BUILDER 7.1 **Compose a New Message**

 In this exercise, you will type and send a new email message. Remember that this is a simulation.

1. Click the **Google Chrome** button on the taskbar at the bottom of your screen.

2. Click in the **address bar**, type `boostyourskills.lablearning.com` and tap Enter and open the chapter resources for your book.

3. Click the **Chapter Resources** tab, click **Chapter 7: Email** to see that section, and then click **Skill Builder 7.1**.

4. Click **Start** to begin the simulation.

   You will complete the rest of the exercise in the simulation.

5. Click the **Close** button.

▶ SKILL BUILDER 7.2 **Check for New Email and Reply to an Email**

 In this exercise, you will check for new email and reply to a new email message.

1. If necessary, return to `boostyourskills.lablearning.com` and open the chapter resources for your book.

2. Click the **Chapter Resources** tab, click **Chapter 7: Email** to see that section, and then click **Skill Builder 7.2**.

3. Click **Start** to begin the simulation.

   You will complete the rest of the exercise in the simulation.

4. Click the **Close** button.

▶ SKILL BUILDER 7.3 **Forward a Message**

Sometimes you will want to send an email message that you received to someone else. In this exercise, you will forward the message from your doctor to a friend.

1. If necessary, return to **boostyourskills.lablearning.com** and open the chapter resources for your book.

2. Click the **Chapter Resources** tab, click **Chapter 7: Email** to see that section, and then click **Skill Builder 7.3**.

3. Click **Start** to begin the simulation.

   You will complete the rest of the exercise in the simulation.

4. Click the **Close** button.

....

▶ SKILL BUILDER 7.4 **Sign Up for Webmail**

In this exercise, you will sign up for real webmail on Gmail. It is free and will look like the simulations you have been using.

NOTE! The Gmail website may not look exactly like the pictures on this page. Sometimes websites change.

1. Open Chrome. If your homepage is not google.com, click in the address bar and then type **google.com** and press ⌐Enter⌐.

2. In the search box, type **create a gmail account** and then press ⌐Enter⌐.

3. Click the **Create a Gmail Account** link in the search results.

4. Click the **Create an Account** button.

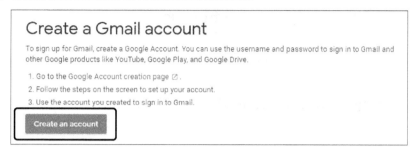

5. Type your information in each box.

6. Write down your username and password because you will need them to sign in to your email.

7. Click **Next**.

   If you did not complete something correctly, Gmail will tell you and you can fix the problem.

8. Follow any additional steps and enter all information needed. Continue until Google tells you, "Welcome." After doing this, you can go to your email account at `mail.google.com` or close Chrome.

 Paired Conversation

With a partner, take turns reading the A and B parts of the conversation.

Partner A	Hi. What are you doing?
Partner B	I'm writing a message to my friend in India.
Partner A	Really? How will you send it?
Partner B	I'll send it to him by email.
Partner A	Is it easy to send an email all the way to India?
Partner B	Yes, it is. It's easy to reply, too.
Partner A	I want to compose and send a question to my doctor, but I don't have email.
Partner B	Well, you can get a webmail account.
Partner A	How much does it cost?
Partner B	Sometimes webmail is free, and it is easy to create an account.
Partner A	Really? Will you help me?
Partner B	Sure. You need to choose a username you want to use for your account.
Partner A	Do I need a password?
Partner B	Yes, you do.
Partner A	Okay. Now tell me what an Inbox is.
Partner B	My Inbox is on the screen now. It shows me a list of the email messages that I received.

Chapter Review

7.1 Identify and Match

Write the correct letter from Column 2 on the line next to the number in Column 1 to create a match.

Column 1

_____ 1. Internet access

_____ 2. Email message

_____ 3. Webmail

_____ 4. Contacts

_____ 5. Email

_____ 6. Gmail

_____ 7. Password

_____ 8. student@gmail.com

Column 2

A. Using this is a fast and easy way to communicate to all people in the world who have Internet access.

B. This company's webmail is one of the most used.

C. This is a sample email address.

D. You must have an email address and this to use email.

E. When you get an email account, you must pick a username and this to access your account.

F. Sending one of these is like sending a letter through the mail.

G. This is useful because you can use it from any computer in the world that has Internet access. Many companies offer it for free.

H. This is a list of names and email addresses in an email address book.

7.2   Answer the Questions

Take some time to think about what you have learned in this chapter.

Exercise A

Write a sentence that answers each question. If you need help, look back in the chapter to find the answer.

1. What is email?

_____

_____

2. Where can you find all the email messages you have received?

_____

_____

3. What are the three parts of an email address?

_____

_____

4. What must you type in at the webmail website to sign into email?

_____

_____

5. What do you click to start a new email message?

_____

_____

6. After you are in your Inbox, what do you click to open an email message?

_____

_____

7. What is it called when you answer one of your email messages?

_____

_____

8. Where do you click to see the messages that you sent?

_____

_____

9. How do you add a person to your contacts?

_____

_____

10. What is the name of a webmail company that will let you sign up for an email address for free?

_____

_____

Exercise B

1. Ask a friend each question and listen to their answers.

2. Have the friend ask you each question and tell them your answers.

CHAPTER 8

Files, Folders, and Windows Search

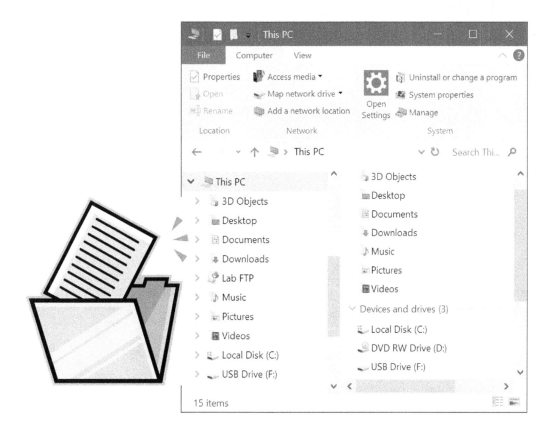

Computer Objectives

■ Use Windows Search to find files and information

■ Work with the File Explorer window and basic file management

■ Save a file and then find and open it later

■ Use double-click to open computer files

Language Objectives

■ Use vocabulary words to describe using files and folders

■ Use vocabulary words to describe parts of the File Explorer window, including files and folders

■ Use computer verbs to describe how to find things using Windows Search

■ Talk with a partner about saving files

■ Talk with a partner about how to play sound files on the File Explorer window

Learning Resources: **boostyourskills.lablearning.com**

 Vocabulary

Picture Dictionary – Nouns

A **noun** is the name of a person, place, or thing. The following nouns are introduced in this chapter:

1. **Folder** – A place where you can organize and keep computer files

2. **Hard drive** – Inside the computer, this holds all computer programs, including Windows; the information stays on the hard drive even after the computer is turned off

3. **File Explorer** – Shows you the storage areas, files, and folders in your computer

4. **C: drive** – A permanent hard drive inside the computer that holds the software that makes your computer work; it can also hold your files

5. **View tab** – A tab on the File Explorer Ribbon with buttons that you can use to change how File Explorer and the files look on the screen

6. **Address bar** – A bar below the File Explorer Ribbon that tells you where you are looking in the computer; the words in this box will change as you look at different things

Computer Verbs

A **verb** tells an action or what a subject is or does. The following verbs are introduced in this chapter:

VERB	MEANING	EXAMPLE
1. **Double-click**	To quickly press and release the left mouse button two times	*Sometimes you need to **double-click** the mouse button to open a window.*
2. **Search**	A program feature that lets you look for a specific topic in your computer	*I forgot how to make the words on my screen look larger. I will **search using** Windows Search to find out how.*
3. **Sort**	To put things in order by name, size, or date	*I have so many files! I'm going to **sort** them by date so I can see which are the newest ones.*
4. **Modify**	To make a small change to text or an object to improve it	*I wrote a letter yesterday, but I need to **modify** it because I thought of one more sentence to write.*
5. **Play**	To listen to a music file or to watch a video file	*Do you want to **play** the new music file that I downloaded from the Internet?*
6. **Choose**	To select (or click on) an option from a group of different choices	*My favorite colors are red, yellow, blue, and green. I will **choose** one for the font in the letter to my friend so it will be brighter.*
7. **View**	To look at an object	*I want to **view** the documents in that folder in different ways, so I will click the View button.*

Concepts and Exercises

The File Explorer Window

In File Explorer, you can see the places where files can be saved. You can also open those places to see the files that are there.

HOW TO OPEN THE FILE EXPLORER WINDOW

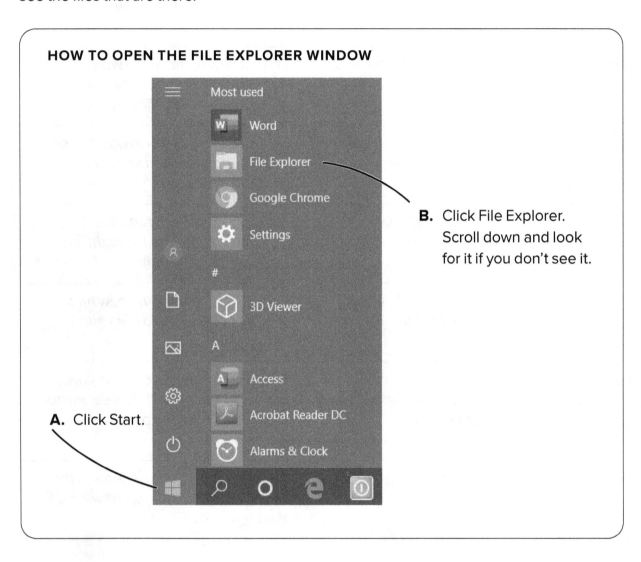

A. Click Start.

B. Click File Explorer. Scroll down and look for it if you don't see it.

When File Explorer opens, you will see all the places where you can save files on the computer.

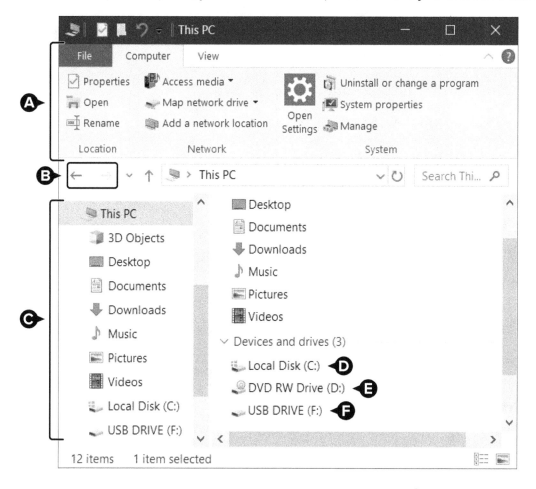

A **Ribbon** – Holds many different commands. As you click on different things in the computer, the commands shown will change.

B **Back and Forward buttons** – Let you to go to folders that you've already opened

C **Navigation pane** – Lets you select different parts of the File Explorer to view the folders and files in each part

D **Hard disk** – The permanent disk inside the computer that holds Windows and other programs

E **DVD drive** – Reads CDs and DVDs (your computer may have a CD drive that does not read DVDs)

F **USB drive** – A small external tool that is inserted into a CPU's USB port so you can save files outside of the computer (your USB drive may have a different name and a different drive letter)

Computers have many places to save information. In this exercise, you will view those different places by looking in File Explorer.

1. Insert your USB drive into the USB port.

2. Open the File Explorer window: **Start→File Explorer**

   If you don't see it, go to Windows System and then choose File Explorer.

3. **Maximize** ☐ the window if it does not fill the screen.

4. Find the Navigation pane.

5. In the File Explorer, find the following:

   - **Documents folder**

   - **C: drive** (your icon may look different)

   - **CD (or DVD) drive**

   - **USB drive E: or F:** (your USB drive may have another name)

6. Leave the File Explorer window open.

Double-Clicking

In File Explorer and on the Windows Desktop, you must double-click with the mouse to open the choices. You always use the left mouse button to double-click.

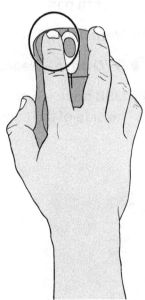

- To see what is in the drives or folders, double-click the left mouse button (press and release two times very fast).

- When you double-click successfully, a window will open to show you what is in that drive or folder.

- After you open the drive or folder, you will see the files and folders inside, if there are any.

In a classroom or other public setting, people usually save information to USB drives because other people will be using the same computers. USB drives can have many different names and different drive letters, but most computers use the E: or F: drive.

HOW TO OPEN USB FILES

A. To see the files on your USB drive, make sure it is inserted into the USB port. Close any new windows that open.

B. Double-click the icon for your USB.

C. You should see your files.

The type of icon each file has tells you in what program the file was made and in which program it will open.

This icon tells you that the file will open in Chrome.

A file with this icon will open in Windows Photos.

This icon tells you that the file was made in Microsoft Word.

Files with this icon are sound or music files.

This is one icon that can be used for video files. Your computer may use a different icon.

▶ EXERCISE 8.2

In this exercise, you will use double-click to open files. You should still be in File Explorer from the last exercise.

1. In the Navigation pane, click **This PC**. In some computers, it may be called something else. In Windows 10, you will see this icon ▭ on the left side of it (you may have to scroll).

2. Double-click the **USB drive** icon on the right side.

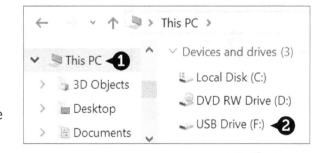

Your USB drive may have another name or letter. Look at the files on your USB drive. Also look at the icon of each file.

3. Double-click each file icon and look at the title bar of the program that opens. Close each program window after you look at it.

4. Click the **Back** ← button to return to the This PC window. Do not close the window.

· ·

Viewing Files on a USB Drive

There are different ways to view files in the File Explorer window using the View tab.

First you must click the View tab on the Ribbon. Then, look in the Layout group.

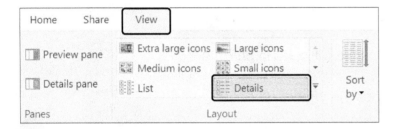

Here are some of the ways that you can view the files:

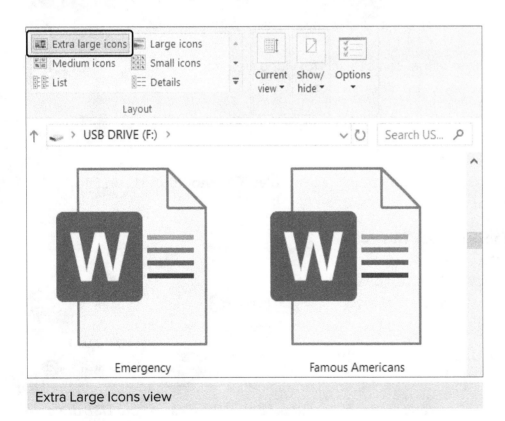

Extra Large Icons view

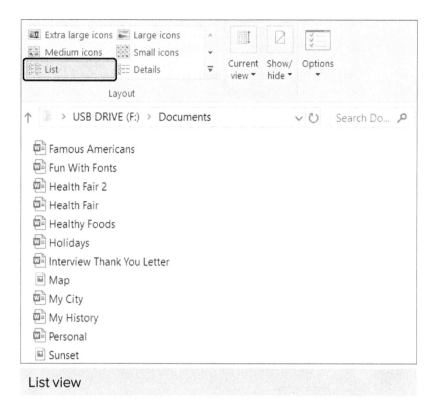

List view

The Details view shows the most information: file name, file size, file type, and more. Notice that the same files are always shown, but the way you view them is a little different.

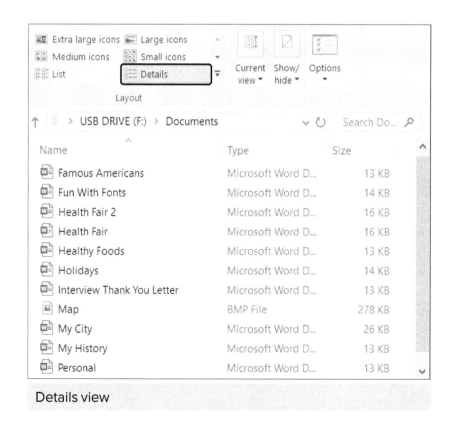

Details view

Sometimes it is helpful to sort your files in alphabetical order by name, by size, or by the date the file was last changed.

If you click the Name heading in Details view, you sort the files in alphabetical order by name.

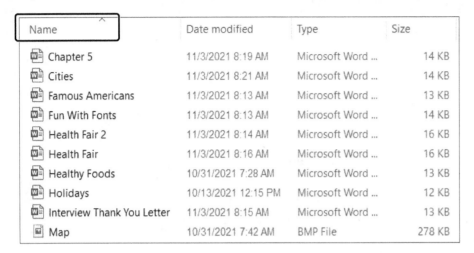

If you click the Size heading in Details view, you sort the files in order by size.

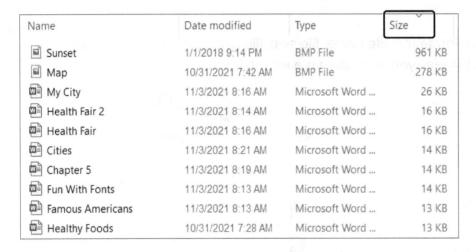

If you click the Date Modified heading in Details view, you sort the files in order by date and time.

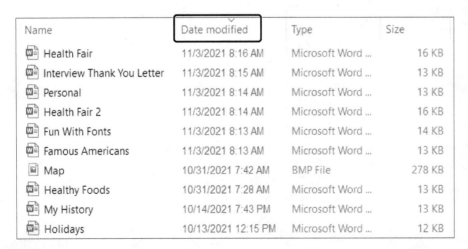

► EXERCISE 8.3

In this exercise, you will look at the files on your USB drive. Write down its name and drive letter, such as "Removable Drive (E:)."

1. If necessary, open File Explorer: **Start→Windows System→File Explorer**

2. Find your USB drive in the Navigation pane. You may have to scroll down to see it.

3. Click the **USB drive** to open it and see all the files on the drive.

4. Click the **View** tab.

5. To see information about your files, click the **Details** button. Look at the size, type, and date of the files.

   Do not worry if you do not have the same files shown here. Your file sizes and dates will be different, too.

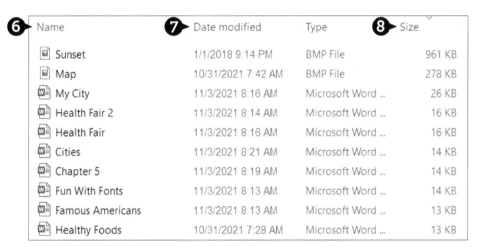

6. Click the **Name** heading to sort the files by name.

7. Click the **Date Modified** heading to sort the files by date.

8. Click the **Size** heading to sort the files by size.

9. Click the **Back** ⬅ button to return to This PC.

   You will see "This PC" or your computer's name in the address bar.

Creating Folders

A folder holds files and other folders in the computer. You can recognize it by its icon.

You can create a folder only when you are in one of the drives in the computer; for example, the C: drive (including in Documents and Pictures) or the USB drive.

HOW TO CREATE A FOLDER

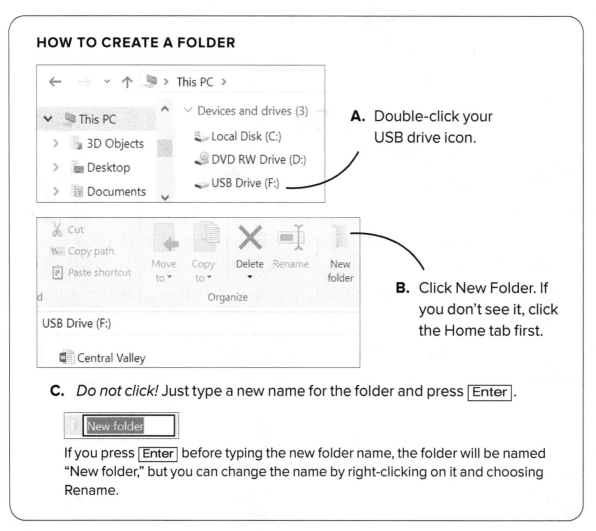

A. Double-click your USB drive icon.

B. Click New Folder. If you don't see it, click the Home tab first.

C. *Do not click!* Just type a new name for the folder and press Enter.

If you press Enter before typing the new folder name, the folder will be named "New folder," but you can change the name by right-clicking on it and choosing Rename.

▶ EXERCISE 8.4

In this exercise, you will create a folder on your USB drive.

1. Click your **USB drive** in the Navigation pane. Scroll down to see it, if necessary.

   A list of the files on your USB drive appears. In the address bar, you will see the name of your USB drive.

2. Click **New Folder**. If you don't see the New Folder button, click the Home tab first.

   The new folder appears.

3. When the New Folder box is created, *do not click* in it. Just type **New Files** and press Enter .

   When you are finished, the folder should look like this:

   Leave File Explorer open.

Opening Files and Saving to a New Location

Sometimes you may want to save a file that you made before to a new location. One of the places you can save a file is into a different folder.

HOW TO OPEN A FILE

  A. First open the program where you created the file.

  B. Choose File→Open→Browse. (In Word, you use the Browse button. In Paint and some other programs, you do not need to use Browse.)

  C. Scroll down the Navigation pane on the left side of the window until you find your USB drive.

  D. Click the icon for your USB drive in the Navigation pane. On the right side, you will see the files on your USB drive.

  E. Double-click the file you want to open.

HOW TO SAVE A FILE TO A NEW FOLDER

  A. Click the File tab.

  B. Click Save As and then click Browse, if necessary. (You do not use Browse in Paint and some other programs.)

  C. Click the new location in the Navigation pane or double-click the folder on the right side of the window to open it. The new location will show in the address bar near the top of the window.

  D. Click Save.

▶ EXERCISE 8.5

In this exercise, you will open a file in Word and then save the file to a new folder. You will then use File Explorer to find the file in the new location.

1. Start Word and then choose **Open→Browse**.

2. Use the Navigation pane to find your USB drive; click it to open it.

3. Double-click the **Chapter 5** file to open it.

   Your original (old) file opens in Word. Now we will save the file in a folder with a new name.

4. Choose **File→Save As→Browse**.

   The files and New Files folder on your USB drive appear on the right side. If not, find the USB drive and click to open it.

5. Double-click the **New Files** folder to open it.

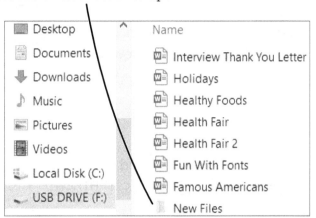

   Notice that now you can see the New Files *folder name in the address bar at the top of the window. That tells you that you are inside the folder.*

6. Click **Save** at the bottom of the window.

   Leave the Word window open. Now we will check to see if we really saved the file into the folder.

7. Choose **Start→File Explorer**.

8. Click the **USB** icon in the Navigation pane.

9. On the right side of the window, double-click the **New Files** folder icon.

   You should see your Chapter 5 file on the right side of the File Explorer window. If you do not, try saving your file again and make sure to save it into the New Files folder. Follow the directions carefully.

10. Close all windows.

. . . .

Taking a Screen Capture

It is sometimes easier to show a picture of the screen to someone than to explain how the screen looks using words. First, you have to capture the screen and paste it into a program, like Paint or Word. Then, you can print it and show the picture of the screen to someone. Some people call this a screenshot. You can also save the screenshot and email it to someone else.

HOW TO TAKE A SCREEN CAPTURE AND SAVE IT IN PAINT

A. Press the Print Screen key. You cannot see it, but a picture of the screen is now on the Clipboard in the computer's memory until you paste it somewhere.

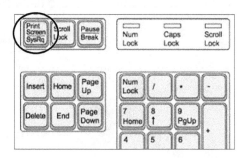

 TIP! The keyboard key to press may be called different things on different keyboards, like Print Screen, PRTSC, or PRTSCN.

B. Open Paint: Start→Paint

C. Click Paste on the left side of the Ribbon.

You will see a picture of the screen in Paint.

D. Choose File→Print→Print.

E. Choose File→Save→Browse

See "Saving Your Work" in Chapter 5, "More with Word," if you need help saving your work. Don't worry if there is another name there; just click and type.

 TIP! To capture the whole screen, use Print Screen. To capture only the window in which you are working, hold down Alt and press Print Screen.

▶ EXERCISE 8.6

In this exercise, you will capture the entire screen, print it, and save it. Then, you will capture the current window, print it, and save it.

1. Start a blank document in Word and then start Calculator.

Your screen should look like this:

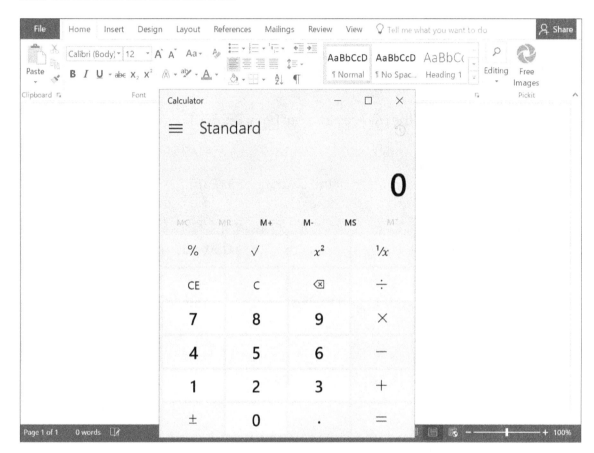

Capture the Full Screen

2. Press the ⎡Print Screen⎤ key.

3. Open Paint.

4. Click **Paste** ⬚ on the left side of the Ribbon.

Now you will see a picture of the entire screen in Paint.

5. Choose **File→Print→Print**.

6. Choose **File→Save**.

7. Type **Screen Capture** in the File Name box.

8. Scroll down the Navigation pane and click your **USB drive**.

9. Double-click the **New Files** Folder to open it. Then, click **Save** on the bottom-right side of the Save As window.

10. Close Paint.

Capture a Window

11. Type some numbers into the Calculator using the keyboard or the mouse.

    Do not click anywhere else.

12. Hold down the ⬚Alt⬚ key and tap ⬚Print Screen⬚.

13. Open Paint and then click **Paste** ⬚ on the left side of the Home tab on the Ribbon.

    You will see a picture of the Calculator in Paint.

14. Print the file.

15. Choose **File→Save** and save the file as **Calculator Capture** in the **New Files** folder.

16. Open File Explorer and then open the window for your USB drive. Double-click the **New Files** folder to open it.

    Look for your new files that you saved. If you do not see them, go back to the Paint window and try saving them again.

17. Close all windows.

....

Windows Search

All computers with Windows 10 come with the Windows Search program. We can type words about the computer, and it will give us information.

(A) Results in files on your computer

(B) Results from the web (Internet)

(C) Search box

You can choose to show the Search box or the Search button on the taskbar. The box or button will appear to the right of the Start button. The Search button looks like a magnifying glass.

HOW TO ADD THE SEARCH BUTTON TO THE TASKBAR

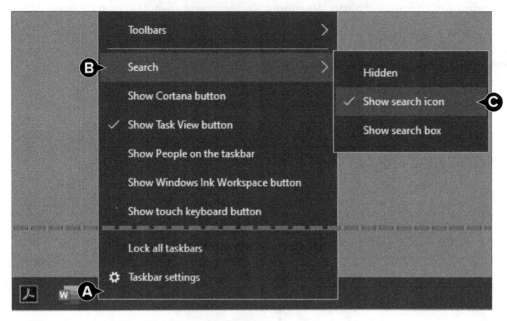

A. Right-click an empty part of the taskbar.

B. Click Search.

C. Click Show Search Icon.

HOW TO USE WINDOWS SEARCH

A. Click the Windows Search button on the taskbar.

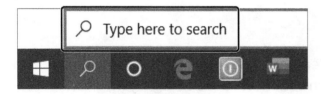

The Search button can also be used to access Cortana. She is a virtual person who you can talk to with a microphone. She is not a real person and is just a part of Windows. We will not use Cortana in this book.

B. In the Search box, type words that describe what you want to read about.

C. Read through the results and click the one you think will give you the best answer. Sometimes the results just will take you to another part of Windows and not give you an answer. If one result does not answer your question, start again and pick another result.

▶ EXERCISE 8.7

In this exercise, you will use Windows Search to find out how to change the desktop background. The background can be a solid color or a picture.

1. Click the **Search** button on the taskbar.

2. In the Search box, type: `change the desktop background`

3. Click the text that reads **Change the desktop background picture**.

4. Read the directions that tell how to change the desktop background. You may be taken to the Internet for this information.

5. Close all windows.

. . . .

◉ Skill Builder Exercises

▶ SKILL BUILDER 8.1 **Use Windows Search**

In this exercise, you will use Windows Search to find information about File Explorer's Ribbon in Windows 10. There is more to learn about it that has not been shown in this book.

1. Open Windows Search: Click the **Search** 🔍 button.

2. In the Search box, type: `File Explorer Ribbon Windows 10`

   You will see a list of places to click that will show you information.

3. Click the link in the results that takes you to the web results.

   > 🕒 file explorer ribbon windows 10 - See web results

4. Now you are on the Internet. Scroll down and look for some videos; click one to watch it.

5. Close all windows.

▶ SKILL BUILDER 8.2 **Save a File to a New Folder**

In this exercise, you will create a new file in Paint, create a new folder, and save the Paint file to the new folder.

Before you begin: Insert your USB drive into the computer.

1. Open the File Explorer window.

2. Scroll down the Navigation pane on the left and click your **USB drive**.

3. Click the **New Folder** button, type **Pictures** as the folder name, and press Enter. Do *not* close File Explorer.

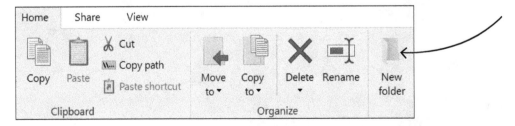

4. Open Paint and draw a picture of a bank close to your house.

5. Choose **File→Save As**.

6. In the File Name box, type **Bank** and then click the **USB icon** in the Navigation pane.

7. Double-click the **Pictures** folder on the right side of the window and then click **Save**.

   The top of the Save As window should look similar to this:

   Now you will check to see if the file was saved in the right place.

8. Click the **File Explorer** icon on the taskbar.

   The files and folders on your USB drive will show.

9. Double-click the **Pictures** folder.

   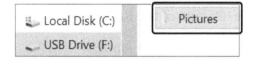

   You should see your Bank file. Look at the icon for your Bank picture. It should look different from the icon for the Word files. If you do not see it, click the icon for Paint on the taskbar and save your file again.

10. Close all windows.

· ·

▶ SKILL BUILDER 8.3 **Play a Music File**

In this exercise, you will play music files. (For this exercise, you will need to turn on the computer speakers before you start.)

1. Open a File Explorer window and click **Music** in the Navigation pane.

   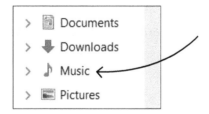

   You may see some music files now. If you see folders, you can double-click to open them to look for music files.

   Look at the type of icon that these files have.

2. Double-click any file with this icon: 🔘

   A sound program will open, and you will hear the music. Different computers may have different icons for sound files.

3. When the song ends, click the **Close** ⊠ button for the sound program.

4. You can listen to other songs by double-clicking the files.

5. When you are finished listening, close all windows.

· ·

▶ SKILL BUILDER 8.4 **Save Screen Captures**

In this exercise, you will make some screen captures, save them, and view them in File Explorer. You will need to insert your USB drive into the computer before you start.

1. Open Weather: **Start→Weather**. You will have to scroll down to the "W" section to find it.

2. Press [Alt]+[Print Screen].

3. Open Paint and click **Paste** 📋 on the left side of the Ribbon.

   Now you will see a picture of the Weather window in Paint.

4. Use **File→Save As** to save the file as **Weather** in the **Pictures** folder on your USB drive. Close Paint.

5. Close Weather.

6. Open Chrome and go to: **www.google.com**

7. Type **Translate** in the search box and then click the **Search** button.

8. Click the **Google Translate** link.

Google Translate
https://translate.google.com/ ▾
Google's free service instantly **translates** words, phrases, and web pages between English and over 100 other languages.

9. Click the drop-down arrow next to *Detect Language* and choose the name of a language that you know and that is not English.

The Google Translate website may look a little different because sometimes it is updated.

10. Click in the big box on the left and type a word in the language you picked.

11. Above the box on the right, click **English** and then click **Translate**.

    You should see the word that you typed in the other language translated to English in the right box now.

12. Press the Print Screen key.

13. Open Paint and click **Paste** ▢ on the left side of the Ribbon.

    You will see a picture of the Google Translate website in Paint.

14. Save the file as **Translate** in the **Pictures** folder on your USB drive.

15. Open a File Explorer window and then open the window for your USB drive.

16. Open the **Pictures** folder and look for your new files. If you do not see them, go back to the Paint window and try saving them again.

17. With the **Pictures** folder open, change the view to **Large Icons**. Make a screen capture and save it as **Large Icons** in the **Pictures** folder.

18. Change the view of the **Pictures** folder to the **Details View**. Capture the screen and save it as **Details View** in your **Pictures** folder.

19. Close all windows.

· ·

Paired Conversation

With a partner, take turns reading the A and B parts of the conversation.

Partner A	Hi. You look like you need help.
Partner B	Yes, I do.
Partner A	What's the problem?
Partner B	I click the icon, but nothing happens.
Partner A	Oh, you have to double-click it.
Partner B	I want to see the files that I saved on my USB drive.
Partner A	Okay. First you have to open File Explorer.
Partner B	How do I do that?
Partner A	Click the Start button, click Windows System, and then click File Explorer. It is on the right side of the Start menu.
Partner B	Okay. Now a File Explorer window is open, but I still don't see my files.
Partner A	You will see them soon. Double-click your USB drive icon.
Partner B	Now I see them! Why do some of them have little Ws on their icons?
Partner A	Well, that is because they were made in Word.
Partner B	Why do we make folders?
Partner A	I like to put my files into folders so they are more organized. It is like putting my clothes in dresser drawers at home.
Partner B	We should play music files today.
Partner A	That sounds like fun!

Chapter Review

8.1   Fill in the Blanks

Write the correct word (or words) in each blank that describes each of the following items. Use your book if you need help.

WORD BANK

USB drive	Ribbon	DVD drive
Navigation pane	Hard disk	Address bar

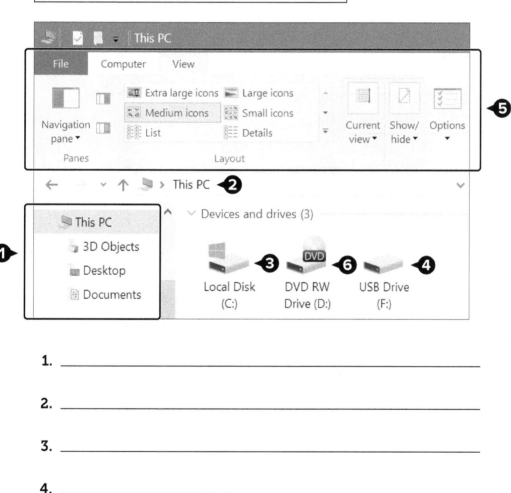

1. _____

2. _____

3. _____

4. _____

5. _____

6. _____

8.2   Verb Worksheet

Fill in the blanks. Select the best answer for each sentence using the computer verbs in the Word Bank. You may use some words more than once.

WORD BANK

Search	view	play	double-click
modify	sort	choose	

1. Sometimes you need to _____ the mouse button to open a window.

2. To _____ is to select something from a group of different things.

3. A program feature that lets you look for something specific is called _____.

4. To put things in order according to name, size, or date is called to _____.

5. I wanted to _____ the date that my documents were made, so I used the View tab.

6. I am going to _____ this music file on my computer.

7. It is fun to _____ my text so it will be better.

. . . .

CHAPTER 9

Writing Letters in Word

Computer Objectives

- Use Microsoft Word
- Write personal and business letters
- Use the Word Ribbon
- Check spelling

Language Objectives

- Use vocabulary words to describe personal and business letters
- Use computer verbs to describe letter writing
- Use computer language to talk about writing letters

 Vocabulary

Picture Dictionary – Nouns

A **noun** is the name of a person, place, or thing. The following nouns are introduced in this chapter:

1. **File tab –** This tab is different from the other Ribbon tabs; click it to open the File menu that lets you open, save, and print documents and do other things

2. **Tab –** A small rectangle on the Word Ribbon that you click to see different groups of buttons

3. **Group –** A set of related buttons that are together in a section under a tab

   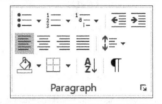

4. **Word Ribbon –** Made of tabs and buttons grouped together

   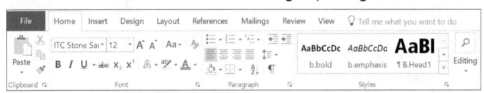

5. **Quick Access toolbar –** The bar that is usually above (but can be below) the Word Ribbon and on the left side; it has buttons that you use often

6. **Spelling & Grammar button –** A tool that checks your spelling and grammar in a document. You can find it on the Review tab.

7. **ScreenTip** – A little box that appears when you put your mouse pointer on a button (without clicking) on the Ribbon; it gives you information about the button	U ▾ abc X₂ X² A ▾ Font **Underline (Ctrl+U)** Underline your text.	
8. **Greeting** – The opening words for a personal letter	Dear Mirna, My Dear Friend, Dear Luis,	
9. **Line and Paragraph Spacing button** – A button in the Paragraph group of the Home tab on the Ribbon that is used to change the space between lines of text	▾	
10. **Salutation** – The opening words of a business letter	Dear Dr. Smith: Dear Ms. Valencia: Dear Governor Grisham:	
11. **Closing** – The last words before you sign a personal letter	Sincerely, Warm regards, With love and friendship,	
12. **Complimentary close** – The last words before you sign a business letter	Sincerely, Respectfully, With appreciation,	

Computer Verbs

A **verb** tells an action or what a subject is or does. The following verbs are introduced in this chapter:

VERB	MEANING	EXAMPLE
1. **Open** (a document)	To put a saved document on the screen	*I need to **open** my document so I can make some changes.*
2. **Ignore**	To pay no attention to something	*I know I made a mistake, but I am going to **ignore** it for now and remember to fix it later.*
3. **Insert**	To put in between two words or objects	*Oh, I forgot to type my middle initial. I need to **insert** it between my first and last names.*
4. **Format**	To make design choices about the way your document looks	*Would you please help me **format** my document so it looks more interesting and professional?*
5. **Check spelling**	To check typed documents to find incorrect spelling and grammar	*I have many mistakes in my letter. I will **check the spelling** now and make the corrections.*
6. **Zoom**	To change the size of the information you see on your screen	*I can't read the information. Let me **zoom** in to make it bigger.*

Concepts and Exercises

....

The Word Window

You first looked at the Word program window in Chapter 2, "Windows and the Start Menu." And you have used Word in several chapters of this book. As you review these pictures, some of the parts will look familiar. New parts of the program window are shown, too.

These pictures may look a little different from the ones on your screen. If you don't see the Ribbon, double-click the Home tab.

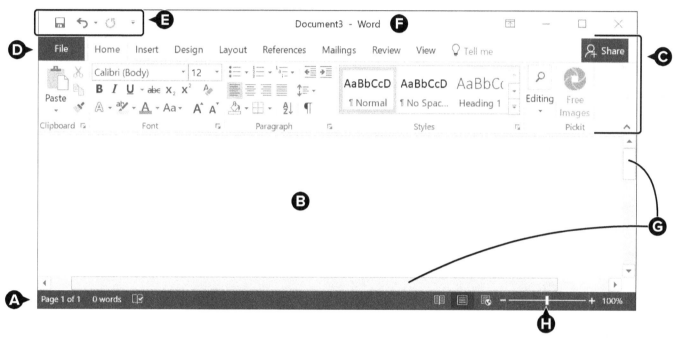

A **Status bar** – Shows important information about your file

B **Work area** – Type your work here

C **Ribbon** – Holds groups of buttons

D **File tab** – Click to open the menu

E **Quick Access toolbar** – Holds commands that are often used

F **Title bar** – Tells you the name of the program you are using

G **Scroll bar** – Lets you move around on the page

H **Zoom control** – Lets you change how big you see the information on your screen

Remember that the Ribbon helps you create documents and change how they look. ScreenTips tell you what the Ribbon buttons do. The Ribbon is organized by tabs and groups. You also saw a Ribbon with tabs and groups in File Explorer.

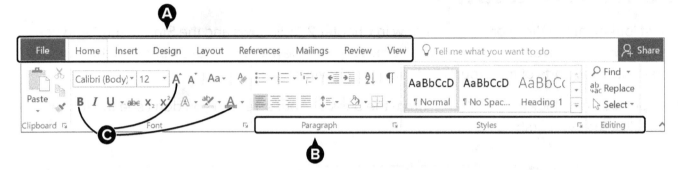

Ⓐ Ribbon tabs – Click each one to use different groups of buttons.

Ⓑ Groups – These are sections of the Ribbon that change with each tab.

Ⓒ Button – This is a small icon that does something when you click it.

Quick Access Toolbar

The Quick Access toolbar is a toolbar on the title bar, either above or below the Ribbon. It is easy to use. You can add or remove buttons from this toolbar, so your Quick Access toolbar may have different buttons than what you see here.

Ⓐ Save button – You click it when you want to save your work.

Ⓑ Undo button – Click this when you want to cancel what you just did.

Ⓒ Redo button – Click this button when you want to bring back what you just did.

You will learn to use the Undo button in Chapter 10, "Editing Word Documents."

ScreenTips

ScreenTips are little boxes that appear when you place your mouse pointer over each button. Every button has its own ScreenTip describing what happens when you click on it.

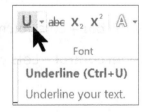

▶ EXERCISE 9.1

In this exercise, you will learn about the Word Ribbon and its parts.

1. Start Word and open a blank document.

2. Click the **Review** tab on the Word Ribbon near the top of the screen.

3. Find (don't click) the Spelling & Grammar button.

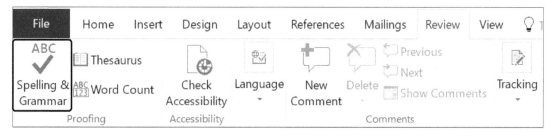

4. Click the **Home** tab.

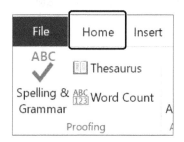

5. Without clicking, put your mouse pointer over each button and read the ScreenTips.

Typing a Personal Letter

A personal letter is a letter that you send to a friend or relative. It is not used for business.

(A)
Melissa Jackson
1223 Appian Way
El Sobrante, CA 94803

(B) March 23, 2021

(C) Dear Jake,

(D) I would like to congratulate you on your new job at the university. You have worked very hard to get this position. I am confident that you will do your very best and have a great deal of success.

I hope that you enjoy your new job and that your supervisor recognizes your talents and rewards you for your excellent work.

(E) Sincerely,

(F) *Melissa*

(G) Melissa

(A) Heading – This part has three lines: name; street address; and city, state, and zip code of the writer. There are two blank lines after the heading.

(B) Date – There should be at least two empty lines after the date.

(C) Greeting – Put a comma after the name of the person you are writing to. Leave an empty line after the greeting.

(D) Body – This is where you put what you want to say in the letter. Leave an empty line after the body of the letter.

(E) Closing – This tells the reader that it is the end of a letter. Put a comma after it. There are three blank lines to leave room for the signature.

(F) Signature – Write your name here with a pen.

(G) Signature line – Type your name here.

▶ EXERCISE 9.2

In this exercise, you will type a personal letter in Word. First you will change the line spacing so your screen matches the pictures in this book. The normal spacing for Word is 1.08. That adds too much space between the lines. We will change it to 1.0 spacing.

1. Click the **Line and Paragraph Spacing** button on the Home tab of the Ribbon.

2. Choose the **1.0** option.

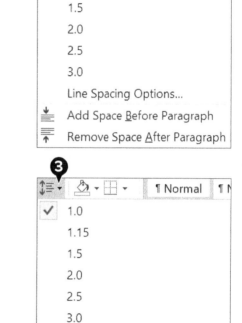

3. Click the **Line and Paragraph Spacing** button again.

   Step 2 closed the menu, so now you must reopen it.

4. Choose **Remove Space After Paragraph**.

5. Type the following personal letter.

   Tap Enter *to add space between the lines.*

🖐 **NOTE!** Your letter may not look exactly like the sample on page 190.

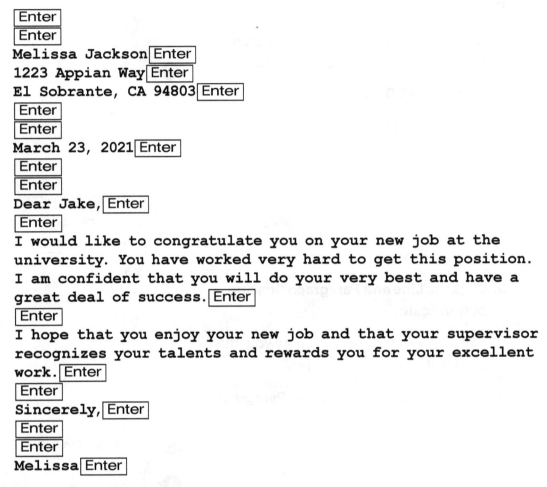

Enter
Enter
Melissa Jackson Enter
1223 Appian Way Enter
El Sobrante, CA 94803 Enter
Enter
Enter
March 23, 2021 Enter
Enter
Enter
Dear Jake, Enter
Enter
I would like to congratulate you on your new job at the
university. You have worked very hard to get this position.
I am confident that you will do your very best and have a
great deal of success. Enter
Enter
I hope that you enjoy your new job and that your supervisor
recognizes your talents and rewards you for your excellent
work. Enter
Enter
Sincerely, Enter
Enter
Enter
Melissa Enter

6. Choose **File→Save As→Browse**.

   The Save As dialog box appears, so you can save your letter.

7. Type **Personal** as the new filename.

8. In the Navigation pane, scroll down and select your **USB drive**.

9. Click the **Save** button.

10. Look at the title bar. You should see the filename there.

🖫 ↺ ▾ ◌ ▾   Personal - Word   🗗   —   🗗   ✕

   Leave the file open.

Checking Your Spelling and Grammar

Microsoft Word comes with a tool that will check the spelling and grammar of your files. The Spelling & Grammar button appears on the Review tab of the Ribbon. When you click it, a dialog box opens. It will show you which words you spelled incorrectly. In this book, we will discuss only spelling changes. You can learn about the grammar changes, underlined in blue, in a more advanced Microsoft Word book.

Ⓐ Word shows you misspelled words as you type. If you see a word in the work area with a wavy red underline, it means the word is not spelled correctly or it is not in Microsoft's English dictionary.

Ⓑ Word will give you some choices of spellings of the word. (In this case there is just one option.) Click the option you think is best.

NOTE! If you can hear your computer's sound, click the speaker ◀)) button to hear the pronunciation of the word.

Ⓒ Click the word in the Suggestions box.

Ⓓ Click Ignore Once if you think the word is spelled correctly.

When you are finished checking the spelling, click in your document.

The Spelling Checker Is Not Always Correct

Sometimes the spelling check feature in Word can make a mistake because it doesn't know the meaning of words. For example, it would see both of these sentences as correct. But are they both correct?

- I red the book.

- I read the book.

▶ EXERCISE 9.3

In this exercise, you will use the Spelling & Grammar command in Word.

Before you begin: Make sure your document called Personal is still open. If not, open it before starting Step 1.

1. Click to the right of the *l* in *congratulate* in the first line of the body of the letter.

   > I would like to congratulate you

2. Tap ⌴ on the keyboard so the word is not spelled correctly.

   A red line will appear under the word to tell you that the word is misspelled. The red line will not show until you click away from the word. Do not pay attention to any other colored lines now. We are only looking at red spelling lines.

3. Click the **Review** tab on the Ribbon.

4. Click the **Spelling & Grammar** button in the Proofing group on the Review tab.

5. Choose the correct word for any spelling mistakes in your letter.

6. Click the **Ignore Once** button if grammar mistakes appear. Grammar mistakes will be underlined in blue.

7. When you are finished, click in your document.

8. Click the **Save** button on the Quick Access toolbar to save the file.

9. Close the file by choosing **File→Close**.

Typing a Business Letter

A business letter is different from a personal letter. It is used to communicate with business people. It is often printed on special paper called letterhead that has the business name and address printed at the top.

Here are the parts of a business letter.

A November 21, 2021

B
Ms. Juanita Thompson
Customer Service Representative
Urbana Software
810 Ivanhoe Way
Urbana, IL 61801

C Dear Ms. Thompson:

D
I would like to thank you for your excellent customer service. You were patient and very helpful.

I have already used your software in my business. It has saved me time and money.

Please send me a list of the other software that you sell.

E Sincerely,

F
Denise Smith
Small Business Owner

A Date – There are four lines inserted on the page before today's date is typed to leave space for a letterhead. There are two blank lines before the inside address.

B Inside address – This is the name and address of the person receiving the letter. There is an empty line after the address and before the salutation.

C Salutation – This part tells who the letter is to. A colon (:) follows the person's name. There is an empty line between the salutation and the body.

D Body – The main part of the letter tells what you want the letter to say. Leave an empty line after the body and before the closing.

E Complimentary close – This comes at the end of the body. The closing is followed by a comma. There must be three empty lines after the complimentary close so the sender can sign their name later.

F Sender's name – The name and title of the sender.

Starting a New Document

Before you can type anything in Word, you must start a new document. To start a new document, you first click the File tab in the top-left corner.

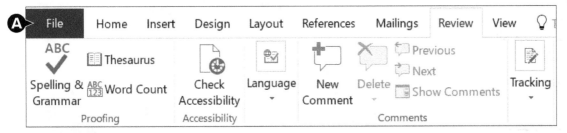

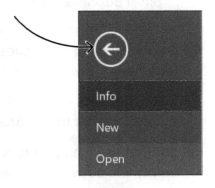

Ⓐ Click the File tab.

Ⓑ Click New.

Ⓒ Click Blank Document.

If you change your mind and want to go back to your Word document without doing anything here, click the Back button.

▶ EXERCISE 9.4

In this exercise, you will type and then save a business letter. This is the type of letter you can use when you are looking for a job.

1. To create a new document, choose **File→New→Blank Document**.

Word creates a new blank document.

2. Click the **Line and Paragraph Spacing** ⫶≡⫶ button and change the spacing to **1.0**. Click the button again and choose **Remove Space After Paragraph**.

3. Type this business letter:

`Enter`
`Enter`
`Enter`
`Enter`
November 21, 2021 `Enter`
`Enter`
`Enter`
Ms. Julia Silvera `Enter`
Superior Solar Company `Enter`
1470 Precision Blvd `Enter`
Atlanta, GA 30303 `Enter`
`Enter`
Dear Ms. Silvera: `Enter`
`Enter`
I am very interested in the receptionist job that your company posted online. I would like this job because your company is exciting and fast growing. It is also much closer to my house than where I work now. `Enter`
`Enter`
At my current job, I have two years of experience working as a receptionist. Customer service is my strongest skill. I treat both customers and coworkers in a professional way. I can handle difficult situations well. `Enter`
`Enter`
You will be pleased with my other skills. I have experience with complicated phone systems and am able to transfer calls to the right person. I have some experience with data entry, including making appointments using the computer. `Enter`
`Enter`
Please consider me for this position. I know that I will easily learn to do other important things working in your office. `Enter`
`Enter`
Sincerely, `Enter`
`Enter`
`Enter`
`Enter`
Sandra Garcia `Enter`

4. Click the **Save** 🖫 button on the Quick Access toolbar and save the file on your USB drive as: **Business**

5. Choose **File→Close**.

Opening a Saved File

You save a file so you can open it later and use it again. This lets you work on the file without needing to retype it.

HOW TO OPEN A SAVED FILE

You can open a saved file like this: File→Open→Browse and then go to the location of the document you want to open.

A. Click the File tab.

B. Click Open.

C. Click Browse.

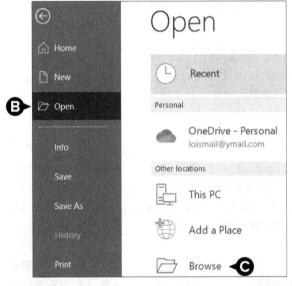

A dialog box will open.

D. Look for your USB drive on the left side of the window. Scroll down if you don't see it at first.

E. Click the location of your file in the Navigation pane, such as the USB drive.

F. Click the file you want to open.

G. Click Open.

▶ EXERCISE 9.5

In this exercise, you will open and print the file you saved in the last exercise. You will preview the document before you print it.

1. Choose **File→Open→Browse**.

2. Click your **USB drive** in the Navigation pane on the left.

3. Click the **Business** file on the right side.

4. Click **Open**.

   Your business letter will appear.

5. Choose **File→Print**.

   On the right side of the window you will see a preview of how your file will look when you print it.

6. When you are finished looking at the document, click the **Print** button on the top-left side.

7. Close Word.

Skill Builder Exercises

▶ SKILL BUILDER 9.1 Type a Personal Letter

In this exercise, you will type a personal letter.

1. Start Word and open a blank document.

2. Click the **Line and Paragraph Spacing** ⬚ button and change the spacing to **1.0**. Click the button again and choose **Remove Space After Paragraph**.

3. Type this personal letter:

`Enter`
`Enter`
Samantha Carison `Enter`
345 Eastern Ave. `Enter`
Lodi, WI 53555 `Enter`
`Enter`
`Enter`
October 20, 2021 `Enter`
`Enter`
`Enter`
Dear Andrea, `Enter`
`Enter`
We are going to have a health fair at school on Saturday, November 13th, at 10 am. I thought that you would like to go, too. You can bring your family. Your family will enjoy it. There will be tests for different diseases, a healthy cooking demonstration, and even fun activities for the children. I know you will have a good time. `Enter`
`Enter`
Please call me to let me know if you and your family will be able to go to the health fair. Our telephone number is (209) 555-6642. Try to let me know by Saturday, November 3rd, so I can get some tickets for you. `Enter`
`Enter`
I look forward to seeing you and your family. Please call me so I can tell you more about it. `Enter`
`Enter`
Sincerely, `Enter`
`Enter`
`Enter`
`Enter`
Samantha `Enter`

4. Check the spelling using the **Spelling & Grammar** ⟨ABC✓⟩ button on the Review tab of the Ribbon.

   ■ Change any words that are not spelled correctly.

   ■ Do not change any of the names.

5. Choose **File→Save As** and save the file as `Health Fair` on your USB drive.

6. Choose **File→Print**.

   On the right side of the window, Word shows what the document will look like when it prints. Look at your letter carefully before you print it.

7. If you need to change something before you print, click the **Back** ⟨←⟩ button to take you out of the Print window so you can make your changes.

8. When you are ready to print, click the **Print** button in the Print dialog box.

9. Choose **File→Close** to close the document but leave Word open.

· ·

▶ SKILL BUILDER 9.2 **Type a Business Letter**

In this exercise, you will type and save a business letter. It is an example of a thank-you letter that people should send after a job interview.

1. Choose **File→New→Blank Document**.

2. Click the **Line and Paragraph Spacing** ⟨↕≡ ▾⟩ button and change the spacing to **1.0**. Click the button again and choose **Remove Space After Paragraph**.

3. Type this business letter:

   `Enter`
   `Enter`
   `Enter`
   `Enter`
   `October 5, 2021` `Enter`
   `Enter`
   `Enter`
   `Mr. Brian Hwang` `Enter`
   `Plumbing Supervisor` `Enter`
   `Expert Plumbing Company` `Enter`
   `1000 Sherwood Place` `Enter`
   `East Brunswick, NJ 08816` `Enter`
   `Enter`
   `Dear Mr. Hwang:` `Enter`
   `Enter`

Thank you for meeting with me to talk about the plumber's
job. I appreciated the opportunity to learn more about
your company and to talk about my job experience and
skills. `Enter`
`Enter`
I would like to become part of your team. I am very
reliable and will work hard to do a good job. One of my best
qualities is my excellent customer service. I hope to hear
from you soon. `Enter`
`Enter`
Thank you for taking the time to interview me. `Enter`
`Enter`
Sincerely, `Enter`
`Enter`
`Enter`
`Enter`
Salil Chauhan `Enter`

4. Click the **Spelling & Grammar** ABC✓ button on the Review tab of the Ribbon.

   - Decide whether to change or ignore what is shown in the dialog box.

   - Change any words that are not spelled correctly.

   - Do not change any of the names.

5. Choose **File→Save As→Browse** and save the file to your USB drive as:
   Interview Thank You Letter

6. Choose **File→Print**.

   Carefully look your letter.

7. If you need to change something before you print, click the **Back** ← button to take you out of the Print window so you can make your changes.

8. When you are ready to print, click the **Print** button inside the Print dialog box.

9. Choose **File→Close**.

▶ SKILL BUILDER 9.3 **Edit a Letter**

In this exercise, you will make changes to your saved Health Fair letter.

1. Choose **File→Open**. Click the **Browse** button, go to your USB drive, and open the **Health Fair** letter you created in Skill Builder 9.1.

2. Make the changes shown in the picture below. Delete the words that are crossed out and add the written words.

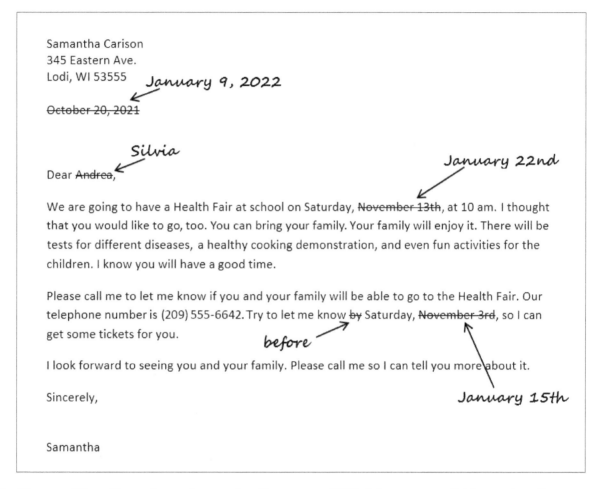

3. Choose **File→Save As** and save the file to your USB drive as: **Health Fair 2**

4. Print the document and then close it.

▶ SKILL BUILDER 9.4   Type a Personal Letter

In this exercise, you will type and save your own personal letter.

1. In a new, blank document, type a personal letter to a friend telling him or her about a new job that you will start soon. You can write about your job now or one that you would like to have.

2. When you finish typing, save the letter to your USB drive with the name: **New Job**

3. Print and then close the letter.

. . . .

▶ SKILL BUILDER 9.5   Type a Business Letter

In this exercise, you will type and save your own business letter.

1. In a new, blank document, type a business letter to your electric company. (Their address should be on your electric bill.) Explain that there is a street light in front of your house that does not work and ask them to fix it.

2. When you finish typing, save the letter to your USB drive with the name: **Street Light**

3. Print and then close the letter. Close Word.

. . . .

 Paired Conversation

With a partner, take turns reading the A and B parts of the conversation.

Partner A	Hi! What's the matter?
Partner B	I'm having trouble writing a letter to my grandma in Word.
Partner A	Why are you having trouble?
Partner B	Well, I can't think of a good greeting.
Partner A	How about "My dearest Grandma"?
Partner B	That sounds good!
Partner A	Well, you don't want it to sound like a business letter!
Partner B	That's true! Personal letters are less formal.
Partner A	You should format your letter so it will look nice.
Partner B	I know. I want a nice font and bigger letters so my grandmother can read it easily.
Partner A	You will need to use the Word Ribbon.
Partner B	I only know a little bit about the Ribbon with all the groups of buttons.
Partner A	Don't worry! If you read the ScreenTips, they will help you to select the changes you need to format your text.
Partner B	Yes, they are very helpful.
Partner A	Have you thought about a closing?
Partner B	I think I will write "Your Loving Granddaughter."
Partner A	That sounds great. Don't forget to check your spelling!
Partner B	I won't! I'll print it and send it to her today.

Chapter Review

9.1 Fill in the Blanks

Write the correct word name in the blank for each part of the Word window.

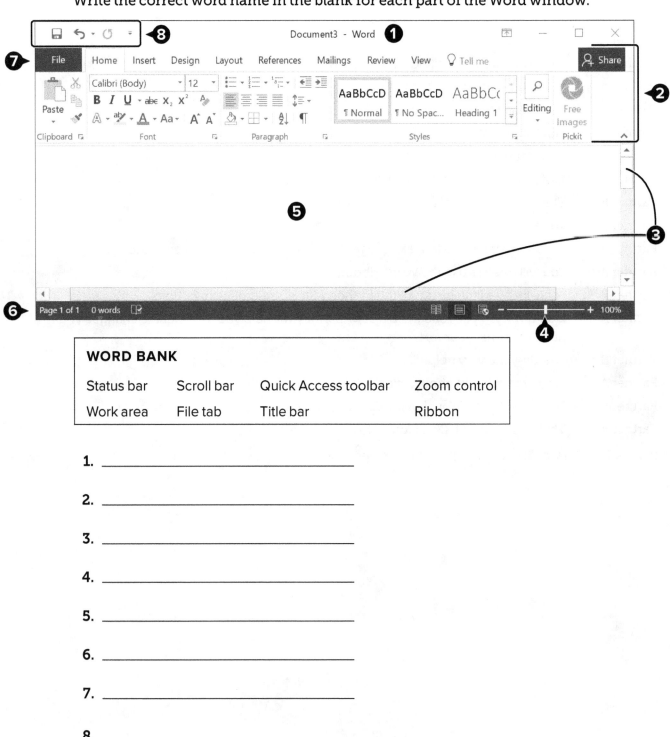

WORD BANK

Status bar	Scroll bar	Quick Access toolbar	Zoom control
Work area	File tab	Title bar	Ribbon

1. _____

2. _____

3. _____

4. _____

5. _____

6. _____

7. _____

8. _____

9.2 Fill in the Blanks

Write a complete sentence that describes each section of the personal letter.

> **❶** Melissa Jackson
> 1223 Appian Way
> El Sobrante, CA 94803
>
> **❷** March 23, 2021
>
> **❸** Dear Jake,
>
> **❹** I would like to congratulate you on your new job at the university. You have worked very hard to get this position. I am confident that you will do your very best and have a great deal of success.
>
> I hope that you enjoy your new job and that your supervisor recognizes your talents and rewards you for your excellent work.
>
> **❺** Sincerely,
>
> **❻** *Melissa*
>
> **❼** Melissa

1. _____

2. _____

3. _____

4. _____

5. _____

6. _____

7. _____

CHAPTER 10

Editing Word Documents

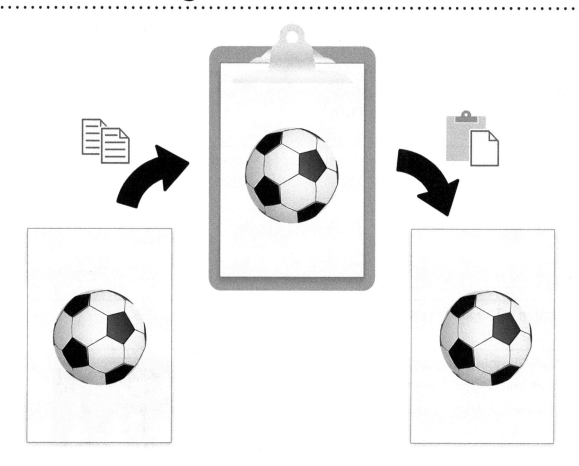

Computer Objectives

- Use Undo
- Use Copy and Paste
- Move from one open program to another
- Create a simple résumé

Language Objectives

- Use vocabulary words to describe how to copy and paste
- Use computer verbs to describe drag and drop, and undo actions
- Explain the parts of a simple résumé to a partner
- Talk with a partner about how to copy and paste

 Vocabulary

Picture Dictionary – Nouns

A **noun** is the name of a person, place, or thing. The following nouns are introduced in this chapter:

1. **Clipboard** – The place in the computer's memory where something goes when you copy it and before you paste it to a new location

2. **Clipboard group** – The part of the Home tab of the Word Ribbon that holds the Cut, Copy, and Paste buttons

3. **Objective** – The kind of job or goal that someone wants

OBJECTIVE
To work in a bank

4. **Skill** – Something you can do that requires learning and practice

5. **Location** – The place where something is

6. **Result** – The effect of a change you make

Before: Learning English is fun.

After: *Learning English is fun.*

7. **Undo button** – A button that allows you to cancel the last thing you did

Computer Verbs

A **verb** tells an action or what a subject is or does. The following verbs are introduced in this chapter:

VERB	MEANING	EXAMPLE
1. **Cut**	To take away or delete text or information you do not want	*I don't like that sentence there. I am going to **cut** it from the first paragraph and paste it in the last paragraph.*
2. **Copy**	To duplicate text in a document so you can put it in a different location	*I will **copy** this sentence from Mr. Smith's letter so I can put it in Mr. Garcia's letter, too.*
3. **Paste**	To take text you copied or cut and put it in a new location	*I copied my address from the first letter. Now I will **paste** it into all the other letters.*
4. **Move**	To change the location of text or other information	*My address is in the wrong place. I will **move** it so it is under my name.*
5. **Undo**	To cancel the last thing you did	*Oops, I made a mistake. I will press the **Undo** button to cancel it.*
6. **Multitask**	To do more than one thing at the same time	*I **multitask** when I cook and talk on the telephone at the same time.*

NOTE! When you cut something, it stays in the memory (Clipboard) so you can paste it somewhere else. When you delete something, you cannot paste it. You can undo both cut and delete actions.

Concepts and Exercises

Typing a Résumé

A résumé is a document you can use to help you find a job. It should have important information about your skills that tells people why they should give you a job. Look at the parts of a résumé below.

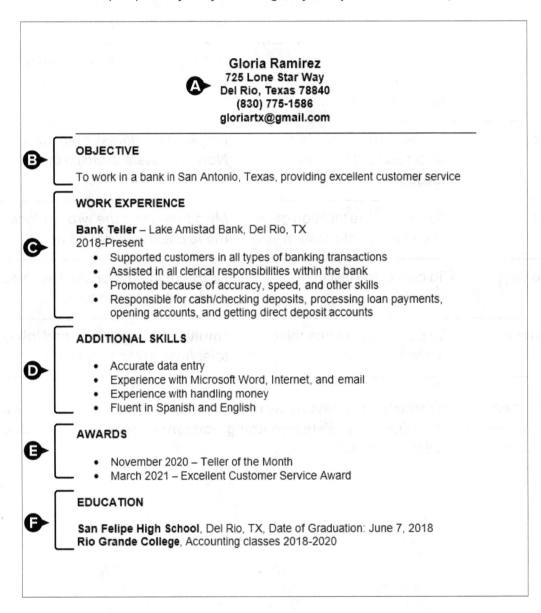

Gloria Ramirez
725 Lone Star Way
Del Rio, Texas 78840
(830) 775-1586
gloriartx@gmail.com

Ⓐ

Ⓑ **OBJECTIVE**

To work in a bank in San Antonio, Texas, providing excellent customer service

WORK EXPERIENCE

Bank Teller – Lake Amistad Bank, Del Rio, TX
2018-Present
Ⓒ
- Supported customers in all types of banking transactions
- Assisted in all clerical responsibilities within the bank
- Promoted because of accuracy, speed, and other skills
- Responsible for cash/checking deposits, processing loan payments, opening accounts, and getting direct deposit accounts

ADDITIONAL SKILLS

Ⓓ
- Accurate data entry
- Experience with Microsoft Word, Internet, and email
- Experience with handling money
- Fluent in Spanish and English

AWARDS

Ⓔ
- November 2020 – Teller of the Month
- March 2021 – Excellent Customer Service Award

EDUCATION

Ⓕ
San Felipe High School, Del Rio, TX, Date of Graduation: June 7, 2018
Rio Grande College, Accounting classes 2018-2020

Ⓐ Put your name, address, phone number, and email address here.

Ⓑ Explain the kind of job you want here.

Ⓒ List the jobs you've had in the past. It is important to include the years, but you do not have to list all the places you have worked.

Ⓓ Put important skills you want the employer to notice here.

Ⓔ List any special recognition that was given to you to show that you are a good worker.

Ⓕ List your high school, college, or other training in the United States or another country.

▶ EXERCISE 10.1

In this exercise, you will type a résumé and then format it to make it look professional.

1. Start Word and open a blank document.

2. Click the **Line and Paragraph Spacing**  button and change the spacing to **1.0**. Then, click the button again and choose **Remove Space After Paragraph**.

   If you need help, look at Exercise 9.2.

3. Type the following résumé. To make the line below the personal information, hold down ⎡Shift⎤ and tap ⎡-⎤ until the line is complete. If your line is too long, use ⎡Backspace⎤ until the line is the right length.

   You must use the text formatting that you learned in Chapter 5, "More with Word." Go back and review how to use the alignment, bold, and bullets buttons.

Gloria Ramirez
725 Lone Star Way
Del Rio, Texas 78840
(830) 775-1586
gloriartx@gmail.com

OBJECTIVE

To work in a bank in San Antonio, Texas, providing excellent customer service

WORK EXPERIENCE

Bank Teller – Lake Amistad Bank, Del Rio, TX
2018-Present
- Supported customers in all types of banking transactions
- Assisted in all clerical responsibilities within the bank
- Promoted because of accuracy, speed, and other skills
- Responsible for cash/checking deposits, processing loan payments, opening accounts, and getting direct deposit accounts

ADDITIONAL SKILLS

- Accurate data entry
- Experience with Microsoft Word, Internet, and email
- Experience with handling money
- Fluent in Spanish and English

AWARDS

- November 2020 – Teller of the Month
- March 2021 – Excellent Customer Service Award

EDUCATION

San Felipe High School, Del Rio, TX, Date of Graduation: June 7, 2018
Rio Grande College, Accounting classes 2018-2020

4. Save the file as **Practice Resume** and then close it.

You will be doing more work with résumés later in this chapter.

Copying and Pasting Within a Program

Sometimes you want to repeat a word or sentence in a document. To save time, you can copy that information instead of typing it again. When you copy something, it goes to a place in the computer's memory that you cannot see, called the *Clipboard*. The computer keeps it there until you copy something else or close the program.

These figures show how the Copy and Paste commands work:

> Melissa Jackson
> 1223 Appian Way
> **Ⓐ** El Sobrante, CA 94803
>
>
> March 23, 2021
>
>
> Dear Jake,
>
> I would like to congratulate you on your new job at the university. You have worked very hard to get this position. I am confident that you will do your very best and have a great deal of success.
>
> I hope that you enjoy your new job and that your supervisor recognizes your talents and rewards you for your excellent work. We look forward to seeing you at the family picnic in **Ⓑ**
>
> Sincerely,
>
> *Melissa*
>
> Melissa

Ⓒ
> I hope that you enjoy your new job and that your supervisor recognizes your talents and rewards you for your excellent work. We look forward to seeing you at the family picnic in El Sobrante.

Ⓐ Select (highlight) what you want to copy then click Copy .

Ⓑ You click where you want to paste what you copied.

Ⓒ After you click the Paste button, the copied text appears.

HOW TO COPY AND PASTE

A. Highlight (select) the information you want to copy.

B. From the Ribbon, choose Home→Clipboard→Copy 📋.

C. Click where you want the information to go.

D. From the Ribbon, choose Home→Clipboard→Paste 📋.

The pasted information stays where it was and also appears in the new location. If any buttons appear automatically, do not click them. They will disappear as you do more work or after you save.

▶ EXERCISE 10.2

In this exercise, you will open, change, and save a personal letter in Word.

1. If necessary, start Word.

2. Choose **File→Open→Browse**. Click the **Personal** file on your USB drive that you made in Chapter 9 and then click **Open**.

3. Highlight **El Sobrante** near the top of the letter.

> Melissa Jackson
> 1223 Appian Way
> El Sobrante, CA 94803

4. From the Ribbon, choose **Home→Clipboard→Copy** 📋.

5. Click at the end of the last paragraph in the body of the letter.

> I would like to congratulate you on your new job at the university. You have worked very hard to get this position. I am confident that you will do your very best and have a great deal of success.
>
> I hope that you enjoy your new job and that your supervisor recognizes your talents and rewards you for your excellent work.
>
> Sincerely,

6. Tap the [Spacebar] to add a space and then type: **We look forward to seeing you at the family picnic in**

Paste the Copied Address

7. Tap the [Spacebar] again then click **Paste** 📋 to paste *El Sobrante* at the end of the sentence you just typed.

8. Type a period to end the sentence. The changed paragraph should look like this:

> I hope that you enjoy your new job and that your supervisor recognizes your talents and rewards you for your excellent work. We look forward to seeing you at the family picnic in El Sobrante.
>
> Sincerely,

Word pastes the copied text into the new position. Don't close this document.

Saving a File with a New Name

Sometimes you want to make changes to a file but still keep the original file not changed. You can keep the old file under the old name and save the new file with the changes using a new name.

HOW TO SAVE A FILE WITH A NEW NAME

   A. Open the file.

   B. Make the changes that you want to make.

   C. Save the changed file using File→Save As→Browse.

   D. Type a new name for the file in the File Name box.

   E. To change the location, click the new place to save the file in the Navigation pane on the left.

   F. Click the Save button.

▶ EXERCISE 10.3

In this exercise, you will make changes to the Personal document and save it with a different filename. This way, you will keep the old file and have the new one, too.

1. Highlight Melissa's name and address at the top of the letter.

> Melissa Jackson
> 1223 Appian Way
> El Sobrante, CA 94803

2. Press ⌈Delete⌋ to remove the highlighted area.

3. Choose **File→Save As→Browse**. Type **Personal2** in the file name box and then click **Save**.

4. Choose **File→Close**.

Undo

You use Undo to cancel the last thing you did. If you just deleted a word and you want to bring it back, you can undo the delete.

This is the button on the Quick Access toolbar that you click to undo.

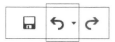

▶ EXERCISE 10.4

In this exercise, you will open the Business file from Chapter 9 and use Cut and Undo. When you use Cut, the information stays in the Clipboard so you can paste it somewhere else if you want.

1. Choose **File→Open→Browse** and open your **Business** file from your USB drive.

2. Highlight the first sentence in the body of the letter.

> Dear Ms. Silvera:
>
> I am very interested in the receptionist job that your company posted online. I would like this job because it is in an exciting and fast-growing company. It is also much closer to my house

3. Click the **Cut** ✂ button in the Clipboard group.

   The highlighted sentence disappears.

4. Click the **Undo** ↶ button.

   The sentence appears again.

5. Click in the first line of the complimentary close between *Sincerely* and the comma.

6. Type a space and the word: **Yours**

7. Click the **Undo** ↶ button.

   The word that you just typed disappears.

8. Save the file as **Business2** and don't close it.

Moving Text in Word

Sometimes the easiest way to move text is to highlight it and then drag it to a new place. This is called drag and drop. It's different from copy and paste because the text does not stay where it was before. It is moved only to the new place.

HOW TO MOVE TEXT IN WORD USING DRAG AND DROP

> Dear Ms. Silvera:
>
> I am very interested in the receptionist job that your company posted online. I would like this job because it is in an exciting and fast-growing company. It is also much closer to my house than where I work now.
>
> At my current job, I have two years of experience as a receptionist. Customer service is my strongest skill. I treat both customers and coworkers in a professional way. I can handle difficult situations well.

A. Highlight the text you want to move and then release the mouse button.

B. Put your mouse on the highlighted area again and then hold down the mouse button.

C. Keep the mouse button down and move your mouse to the new place for your text.

D. Release the mouse button.

This symbol shows you where the text will go.

Your mouse pointer will look like this when moving text.

▶ EXERCISE 10.5

In this exercise, you will use the drag-and-drop method to move the last sentence up to the first paragraph and then undo the action.

1. Highlight the second paragraph of the letter. Release the mouse button.

Dear Ms. Silvera:

I am very interested in the receptionist job that your company posted online. I would like this job because it is in an exciting and fast-growing company. It is also much closer to my house than where I work now.

At my current job, I have two years of experience as a receptionist. Customer service is my strongest skill. I treat both customers and coworkers in a professional way. I can handle difficult situations well.

---

2. Put your mouse on the highlighted area again and hold down the mouse button.

3. Drag the paragraph to the beginning of the first paragraph of the letter. Release the mouse button.

See that the paragraph is at the new location, as shown here:

Dear Ms. Silvera:

At my current job, I have two years of experience as a receptionist. Customer service is my strongest skill. I treat both customers and coworkers in a professional way. I can handle difficult situations well.
I am very interested in the receptionist job that your company posted online. I would like this job because it is in an exciting and fast-growing company. It is also much closer to my house than where I work now.

---

4. Click the **Undo** ⟲ button on the Quick Access toolbar to put the paragraph back where it was.

5. Choose **File→Close**.

6. Choose **No** if asked whether you want to save your changes.

Right-Click to Copy and Paste

Sometimes it is easier to copy and paste by clicking the right mouse button. For example, if you want to paste the text far away from where you copied it, it is easier to use the mouse button.

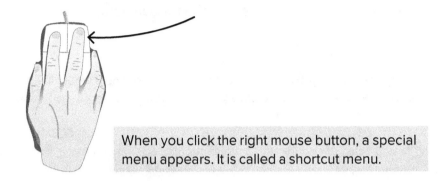

When you click the right mouse button, a special menu appears. It is called a shortcut menu.

HOW TO COPY USING A RIGHT-CLICK AND THE SHORTCUT MENU

A. Holding down the left mouse button, highlight what you want to copy.

B. Release the left button and then press down the right button in the highlighted area and release it. The shortcut menu will appear.

C. Click Copy with the left mouse button.

D. Click where you want the information to go in the document you are in or in a different one.

E. Right-click to show the shortcut menu.

F. With the left button, click Paste. (Or choose Home→Clipboard→Paste from the Ribbon.)

In this exercise, you will use right-click and the shortcut menu to copy and paste text.

1. Choose **File→Open→Browse** and open the **Business** file from your USB drive.

   Now you will copy some text.

   I am very interested in the receptionist job that your company posted online. I would like this job because it is in an exciting and fast-growing company. It is also much closer to my house than where I work now.

   ❷ At my current job, I have two years of experience as a receptionist. Customer service is my strongest skill. I treat ❸ th customers and coworkers in a professional way. I can handle difficult situations well.

   - ✂ Cut
   - ❹ 📋 Copy
   - 📋 **Paste Options:**

2. Highlight the second paragraph in the body of the letter. Release the left mouse button.

3. Put your mouse on the highlighted area and right-click.

   See that the shortcut menu shows now.

4. Click **Copy** with the left mouse button.

   Word copies the highlighted text. The letter has not changed.

5. With the left button, click below the date near the top of the letter.

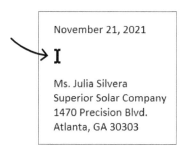

   November 21, 2021

   I

   Ms. Julia Silvera
   Superior Solar Company
   1470 Precision Blvd.
   Atlanta, GA 30303

6. Right-click in the same place to bring up the shortcut menu. Click **Paste** with the left button.

   - ✂ Cut
   - 📋 Copy
   - 📋 **Paste Options:**

Now you will see the sentence copied below the date, as in this figure.

> November 21, 2021
> At my current job, I have two years of experience working as a receptionist. Customer service is my strongest skill. I treat both customers and coworkers in a professional way. I can handle difficult situations well.

7. Highlight the sentences you just pasted below the date and press Delete.

8. **Save** 🖫 the **Business** file.

9. Choose **File→Close**.

   Word closes the document but leaves the Word program open.

10. Choose **File→New→Blank Document**.

    Word creates a new, blank document for the next exercise.

. . . .

Copying from One Program to Another

You have more choices with the files you make if you can copy information from one program and paste it into another. You can copy pictures and text.

HOW TO COPY FROM ONE PROGRAM AND PASTE INTO ANOTHER

A. Open the file in the program with the text you want to copy (for example, some text in Chrome).

B. Find and select what you want to copy.

C. Click the Copy 📋 button. If the program does not have a Copy button, right-click on the highlighted text and then click Copy.

D. Open the program where you want to paste (for example, Word). (This is called multitasking.)

E. Click where you want the information to go.

F. Click the Paste button. If the program does not have a Paste button, right-click and then click Paste.

▶ EXERCISE 10.7

In this exercise, you will do a calculation on the Calculator program, copy the answer, and paste the answer into Word.

1. Start Calculator.

2. Follow these steps to multiply 56 by 10:

    A. Click the **5** button and then the **6** button. You can see the number appear in the number box near the top of the calculator.

    B. Click the **multiplication (X) sign**.

    C. Click the **1** button and then the **0** button.

    D. Click the **equals** (=) **sign** to finish.

    You can see the answer (560) in the number box.

3. Right-click your answer in Calculator and choose **Select All**. Then right-click the number again and choose **Copy**.

    You cannot use the Copy button because the calculator does not have one.

4. Click the **Word** button on the Windows taskbar at the bottom of the screen.

    The new blank document that you made at the end of the last exercise should be open.

5. Type this sentence: `My answer from the calculator is`

6. Click the **Paste** button and then type a period at the end of the sentence.

    Your result should look like this: My answer from the calculator is 560.

7. Save the file as **Answer** on your USB drive.

8. Close the Word program.

    Use the Close button on the Word title bar.

9. Close the Calculator program.

Skill Builder Exercises

▶ SKILL BUILDER 10.1 **Move Text by Dragging**

In this exercise, you will open a file and then move text in it using drag and drop.

1. Start Word and open the **Practice Resume** file you created in Exercise 10.1 from your USB drive.

2. Highlight the *EDUCATION* section and the line of space below it and then release the mouse button.

AWARDS

- November 2020 – Teller of the Month
- March 2021 – Excellent Customer Service Award

EDUCATION

San Felipe High School, Del Rio, TX, Date of Graduation: June 7, 2018
Rio Grande College, Accounting classes 2018-2020

---

3. Move your mouse onto the highlighted area and hold down the left mouse button.

4. Keep the mouse button down and drag until you see a small dashed line in front of *AWARDS*. Release the mouse button.

After you have moved the paragraph, the letter should look like this:

ADDITIONAL SKILLS

- Accurate data entry
- Experience with Microsoft Word, Internet, and Email
- Experience with handling money
- Fluent in Spanish and English

EDUCATION

San Felipe High School, Del Rio, TX, Date of Graduation: June 7, 2018
Rio Grande College, Accounting classes 2018-2020

AWARDS

- November 2020 – Teller of the Month
- March 2021 – Excellent Customer Service Award

---

5. Save the file as **Practice Resume 2**. Do *not* close the file.

▶ SKILL BUILDER 10.2 Use Undo

In this exercise, you will use the Undo button to reverse changes to your document. The Practice Resume 2 file should still be open.

1. Highlight all of the personal information section at the top of the document.

2. From the Ribbon, choose **Home→Clipboard→Cut** ✄.

3. Click the **Undo** ↶ button on the Quick Access toolbar to bring it back.

4. Highlight Gloria's telephone number in the personal information section and type your phone number to replace it.

5. Click **Undo** ↶ to change it back.

6. Close Word. If a message appears asking if you want to save the file, click **No**.

. . . .

▶ SKILL BUILDER 10.3 Copy a Picture from the Internet into Word

In this exercise, you will find a picture to copy. Then you will copy it and paste it into Word.

1. Open Chrome and, if necessary, type **google.com** in the address bar and press ⌷Enter⌷.

2. Click the **Images** link.

3. In the Search box, type the name of the city and state where you live and then click the **Search** button.

Google displays pictures found by your search. Now you will copy a picture.

4. Look at the pictures from the search results.

Google displays a larger view of the picture with some other smaller ones.

5. Right-click the picture. (You will see a shortcut menu.)

6. Left-click **Copy Image** in the shortcut menu.

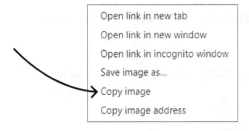

7. Open Word and start a blank document. Type the name of your city and press Enter.

8. Type four sentences about the city or area where you live.

9. From the Ribbon, choose **Home→Clipboard→Paste**.

10. Save your file as **My City** on your USB drive.

11. Print the file and then close the window.

Make a Document About an Emergency Vehicle

In this exercise, you will create a Word document about an emergency vehicle. First you will find a picture, copy it, and paste it into your Word document. Below the picture, you will type some information about the emergency vehicle. Then you will save and print the document.

1. Use Google to find and copy a picture of a police car, a fire truck, or an ambulance.

2. Paste the picture into Word. Press the **right arrow** → key on the keyboard and then press Enter to get to the next line under the picture.

3. Type the name of the emergency vehicle you copied and press Enter.

4. Type one paragraph that tells about the kinds of emergencies that vehicle is used for.

5. Save the file on your USB drive as: **Emergency**

6. Print the file and then close Word.

Complete this form to organize your information to write your résumé. Use another piece of paper if necessary.

Personal Information

Complete name: _____

Address: _____

Telephone number: _____

Email address: _____

Objective

Explain the kind of job that you want: _____

Work Experience

List the job you have now or the last job you had.

Job title: _____

Company: _____

Years worked: _____

Things that you did at that job: _____

Write the same information for other jobs you have had that are related to the job you are looking for.

Additional Skills

Describe job skills that you want the employer to notice:

_____

_____

Awards

List any special recognition given to you because you were a good worker:

_____

Education

List high school, college, or other training in the U.S. or another country:

_____

▶ SKILL BUILDER 10.6 **Create Your Résumé**

In this exercise, you will create your own résumé in Word using the worksheet you completed in Skill Builder 10.5.

1. Start Word and open a new document.

2. Use the **Line and Paragraph Spacing** button twice to change the spacing to **1.0** and then click **Remove Space After Paragraph**.

3. Type your personal information centered so it looks like the sample résumé.

4. Hold down [Shift] and tap [-] to make a line under your personal information.

5. Type your Objective, Work Experience, Additional Skills, Awards, and Education sections into Word.

6. Read over your work carefully. Make any changes and corrections.

7. Save your résumé to your USB drive using your name as the filename.

8. Print your résumé and then read it again to check it. Have someone else read it and tell you what they think about it.

9. Make any changes that you need to make and then save your résumé again. If you made changes, print the file again.

10. When you are finished, close all windows.

 Paired Conversation

With a partner, take turns reading the A and B parts of the conversation.

Partner A	Greetings, my friend!
Partner B	Hi! Are you ready for our computer chapter today?
Partner A	Yes. I have so many files that I need to work on.
Partner B	That's great. We can multitask today.
Partner A	What's multitasking?
Partner B	It means working with two or more programs at the same time.
Partner A	Oh, that's a good word. Is task a word that means a job that you need to do?
Partner B	Yes. Today we will learn how to copy to the Clipboard.
Partner A	And then we will paste the information somewhere else, right?
Partner B	That's right. We'll also learn how to cut text and move it.
Partner A	I really need to learn how to cut and move text!
Partner B	Cut, Copy, and Paste are all on the Clipboard group.
Partner A	Is the Clipboard group on the Word Ribbon?
Partner B	Yes! You seem to understand this stuff.
Partner A	Thanks. I know the location of the files I want to work on.
Partner B	Good. When you finish, make sure to type a filename in the File Name box and save your new file to your USB drive.
Partner A	Great! I'll remember where I saved it.
Partner B	You're learning so quickly. Soon you can use these skills to search for a job.

# Chapter Review

10.1 Fill in the Blanks

Fill in the blanks. Select the best answer for each blank using the vocabulary words in the Word Bank. The sentences describe how to copy and paste.

WORD BANK

highlight	Copy	Paste	click
Clipboard	save	location	Word Ribbon

1. To copy information, you must _____ it first.

2. To copy, click the _____ button on the Home tab

   of the _____.

3. You will not see anything happen yet. The information you copied is now in a place

   on the computer called the _____.

4. Now, _____ where you want the information to go.

5. Then, click the _____ button on the Home tab of the Ribbon to put

   the information into your document.

6. If you see any other buttons appear automatically, do not click them. They will go

   away as you do more work or after you _____ the file.

7. The pasted information stays where it was, and it also goes to the

   new _____.

10.2 Paired Conversation and Language Practice

Fill in the blanks in the conversation below using the words in the Word Bank. You can use a word more than once, if necessary. Then, circle all pronouns used in the conversation. Finally, with a partner, take turns reading the A and B parts of the conversation.

TIP! Pronouns take the place of nouns.

> **WORD BANK**
>
> | Greetings | chapter | files | multitask | multitasking |
> |---|---|---|---|---|
> | Clipboard | paste | cut | move | copy |
> | Clipboard group | location | File Name box | | |

Partner A	_____, my friend!
Partner B	Hi! Are you ready for our computer _____ today?
Partner A	Yes. I have so many _____ that I need to work on.
Partner B	That's great. We can _____ today.
Partner A	What's _____?
Partner B	It means working with two or more programs at the same time.
Partner A	Oh, that's a good word. Is task a word that means a job that you need to do?
Partner B	Yes. Today, we will learn how to copy to the _____.
Partner A	And then we will _____ the information somewhere else, right?
Partner B	That's right. We'll also learn how to _____ text and move it.
Partner A	I really need to learn how to cut and _____ text!
Partner B	Cut, _____, and Paste are all on the Clipboard group.
Partner A	Is the _____ _____ on the Word Ribbon?
Partner B	Yes! You seem to understand this stuff.
Partner A	Thanks. I know the _____ of the files I want to work on.
Partner B	Good. When you finish, make sure to type a filename in the _____ _____ _____ and save your new file to your USB drive.
Partner A	Great! I'll remember where I saved it.
Partner B	You're learning so quickly. Soon you can use these skills to search for a job.

· ·

Chapter Review Answer Key

Chapter 1: About Computer Basics

1.1	Fill in the Blanks
1.	CPU
2.	Monitor
3.	Speakers
4.	Keyboard
5.	Mouse

1.2	Verb Worksheet
1.	shut down
2.	turn on
3.	click
4.	let go
5.	select
6.	press
7.	turn off
8.	drag
9.	go to

1.2	Fill in the Blanks
1.	Sit up straight in your chair.
2.	Keep your wrists straight.
3.	The top of the monitor should be at the same level as your eyes.
4.	Sit with your feet flat on the floor.

Chapter 2: Windows and the Start Menu

2.1	Fill in the Blanks
1.	Icons
2.	Start button
3.	Desktop
4.	Mouse pointer
5.	Taskbar

2.2	Fill in the Blanks
1.	Title bar
2.	Ribbon
3.	Work area
4.	Minimize
5.	Maximize
6.	Close

2.3	Fill in the Blanks
1.	Start, Word
2.	No answer needed
3.	Minimize, Maximize, Close
4.	Maximize, Restore
5.	No answer needed
6.	Minimize
7.	Word
8.	Title bar

Chapter 3: Windows Programs

3.1	Verb Worksheet
1.	You can <u>preview</u> a document to see how it will look when you print it.
2.	To <u>appear</u> is when an object shows on the screen and you can see it.
3.	To uncheck a box is called to <u>clear</u> it.
4.	To <u>check</u> means to click the box so that a checkmark appears.
5.	To look at something is to <u>view</u> it.
6.	To <u>play</u> means to use a computer game.
7.	To keep your finger pressed on the mouse button is to <u>hold</u> the button.
8.	To <u>release</u> means to take your finger off of the mouse button.
9.	To <u>let up</u> means to release or let go of a button.

3.2	Fill in the Blanks

Exercise A: Add Two Numbers

1.	Click the first <u>number</u>.
2.	Click the <u>plus</u> sign.
3.	Click the <u>second number</u>.
4.	Click the <u>equals</u> sign.

Exercise B: Multiply Two Numbers

1.	Click the first <u>number</u>.
2.	Click the <u>X</u> sign.
3.	Click the <u>second number</u>.
4.	Click the <u>equals</u> sign.

Chapter 4: Creating a Document in Word

4.1	Fill in the Computer Keyboard

Write keyboard letters, symbols, and numbers on the keyboard figure. Then, draw hands on the keyboard figure with the fingers on the correct keys.

4.2	Identify and Match
1.	D
2.	F
3.	E
4.	B
5.	C
6.	A

Chapter 5: More with Word

5.1	Fill in the Blanks
1.	USB port
2.	insert, easily, turn
3.	Taskbar, bottom
4.	Eject
5.	safe

5.2	Verb Worksheet
1.	align
2.	save
3.	format
4.	insert
5.	decrease
6.	highlight
7.	right-click
8.	scroll
9.	increase

Chapter 6: The Internet

6.1	**Fill in the Blanks**
1.	back button
2.	address bar
3.	menu button
4.	scroll bar

6.2	**Paired Conversation and Language Practice**
Partner A	I'm a new student.
Partner B	Welcome to our classroom!
Partner A	I heard that today's class is about the Internet.
Partner B	That's right.
Partner A	Which websites will we visit?
Partner B	I'm not sure. We'll have to use a search engine.
Partner A	Is that what you use to look for things on the Internet?
Partner B	That's right.
Partner A	Well, let's visit an interesting website.
Partner B	I know! Let's go to our school's homepage first.
Partner A	That's a great idea. Let's connect to it now.
Partner B	Well, let's type the Internet address for our school in the address bar.
Partner A	Okay. Now what do I do?
Partner B	We can use the links to go to the pages we want.
Partner A	Thanks. Now I want to browse the Internet.
Partner B	You'll have to wait. We have to do a simulation exercise first.
Partner A	Okay.
Partner B	Later, we can search for other interesting subjects.

Chapter 7: Email

7.1	**Identify and Match**
1.	D
2.	F
3.	G
4.	H
5.	A
6.	B
7.	E
8.	C

7.2 Answer the Questions

These are just example answers.

1.	Email is a way to send messages and information from one computer to another through the Internet.
2.	Email messages that I receive from other people are in the Inbox.
3.	The three parts of an email address are the username, the at (@) symbol, and the email service provider.
4.	To sign into my email account, I must type in (or enter) my password.
5.	To start a new email message, I click the Compose button.
6.	I can open an email message by clicking its subject line.
7.	To answer an email message is to "reply" to it.
8.	To see the email messages that I have sent to other people, I click Sent.
9.	To add a person to my contacts, I click Contacts and enter their name and email address.
10.	Google offers the free webmail service Gmail.

Chapter 8: Files, Folders, and Windows Search

8.1	Fill in the Blanks
1.	Navigation pane
2.	Address bar
3.	Hard disk
4.	USB drive
5.	Ribbon
6.	DVD drive

8.2	Verb Worksheet
1.	double-click
2.	choose
3.	Search
4.	sort
5.	view
6.	play
7.	modify

Chapter 9: Writing Letters in Word

9.1	Fill in the Blanks
1.	Title bar
2.	Ribbon
3.	Scroll bar
4.	Zoom control
5.	Work area
6.	Status bar
7.	File tab
8.	Quick Access toolbar

9.2	Fill in the Blanks

Your sentences may vary but should include these words.

1.	Heading
2.	Date
3.	Greeting
4.	Body
5.	Closing
6.	Signature
7.	Signature line

Chapter 10: Editing Word Documents

10.1 **Fill in the Blanks**	
1.	Highlight
2.	Copy, Word Ribbon
3.	Clipboard
4.	Click
5.	Paste
6.	Save
7.	Location

10.2 **Paired Conversation and Language Practice**	
Partner A	Greetings, my friend!
Partner B	Hi! Are you ready for our computer chapter today?
Partner A	Yes. I have so many files that I need to work on.
Partner B	That's great. We can multitask today.
Partner A	What's multitasking?
Partner B	It means working with two or more programs at the same time.
Partner A	Oh, that's a good word. Is task a word that means a job that you need to do?
Partner B	Yes. Today we will learn how to copy to the Clipboard.
Partner A	And then we will paste the information somewhere else, right?
Partner B	That's right. We'll also learn how to cut text and move it.
Partner A	I really need to learn how to cut and move text!
Partner B	Cut, Copy, and Paste are all on the Clipboard group.
Partner A	Is the Clipboard group on the Word Ribbon?
Partner B	Yes! You seem to understand this stuff.
Partner A	Thanks. I know the location of the files I want to work on.
Partner B	Good. When you finish, make sure to type a filename in the File Name box and save your new file to your USB drive.
Partner A	Great! I'll remember where I saved it.
Partner B	You're learning so quickly. Soon you can use these skills to search for a job.